MW01444093

A Deep River Year

People, Passages, and Promises

TIMOTHY E. HAUT

WESTBOW
PRESS®
A DIVISION OF THOMAS NELSON
& ZONDERVAN

Copyright © 2019 Timothy E. Haut.

All rights reserved. No part of this book may be used or reproduced by any means, graphic, electronic, or mechanical, including photocopying, recording, taping or by any information storage retrieval system without the written permission of the author except in the case of brief quotations embodied in critical articles and reviews.

This book is a work of non-fiction. Unless otherwise noted, the author and the publisher make no explicit guarantees as to the accuracy of the information contained in this book and in some cases, names of people and places have been altered to protect their privacy.

WestBow Press books may be ordered through booksellers or by contacting:

WestBow Press
A Division of Thomas Nelson & Zondervan
1663 Liberty Drive
Bloomington, IN 47403
www.westbowpress.com
1 (866) 928-1240

Because of the dynamic nature of the Internet, any web addresses or links contained in this book may have changed since publication and may no longer be valid. The views expressed in this work are solely those of the author and do not necessarily reflect the views of the publisher, and the publisher hereby disclaims any responsibility for them.

Any people depicted in stock imagery provided by Getty Images are models, and such images are being used for illustrative purposes only. Certain stock imagery © Getty Images.

Photos by Phyllis Bjornberg-Haut

ISBN: 978-1-9736-7979-0 (sc)
ISBN: 978-1-9736-7980-6 (hc)
ISBN: 978-1-9736-7978-3 (e)

Library of Congress Control Number: 2019918687

Print information available on the last page.

WestBow Press rev. date: 12/11/2019

Contents

Introduction ix

January 1
    Sparrows' New Year 3
    Cold 7
    The Empty Chairs 11
    The Zen of Cats 15
    Seeds 19

February 23
    February, Stillness 25
    Love 29
    Ice 33
    Blue Irises 37

March 41
    Ash Wednesday 43
    Signs 47
    St. Joseph's Day 51
    Holy Ground 55
    Peepers and Peas 59

April 63
    Wren's Song 65
    Sun Dog 69
    Easter Hands 73
    May Day 77

May 81
    Bubble 83
    Lilacs 87
    Family Reunion 91
    Memorial Day 95

June 99
    Jack-in-the-Pulpit 101
    Heart Berries 105
    Pomp and Circumstance 109
    June Night 113

July 117
    Fireworks 119
    A Baseball Dream 123
    Summer Rain 127
    Comes the Parade 131
    First Tomato 135

August 139
    Mountaintop 141
    Shooting Stars 145
    Summer Afternoon 149
    Fair 153

September 157
    Carry Me Home, Old River 159
    Girl on the Bus 163
    Promise 167
    Morning Walk 171

October 175
    Woolly Bear 177
    Train Tracks 181
    Autumn Crown 185
    Morning Glory 189
    Ghoulie Girl 193

November 197
    Bittersweet 199
    Wood, Split 203
    Birthday 207
    A Song to Slip from the Heart 211

December 215
    Red 217
    Christmas Tree 221
    Hearth Fire 225
    Somewhere a Star 229
    The Last Day 233

Introduction

Deep River is a small town on the beautiful Connecticut River. It was a part of the original Saybrook Colony, a refuge for Puritans seeking a sanctuary in the New World in 1635 along the coast of New England. Later their descendants traveled upstream and found this little place with swift-running streams and good land, and they built factories and businesses that shared a reputation for Yankee industry. Today outside the triangular brick Town Hall in the center of town is a statue of an elephant—a reminder of the ivory trade that brought thousands of elephant tusks from Africa to be made into piano keys, billiard balls, buttons and combs for the burgeoning markets of America. Those factories are no longer here, and our little town has tried to atone for the destruction of those beautiful creatures by building a more gentle and peaceful presence in the world.

Deep River is my town, my home. And here I watch the seasons come and go. Here my children have gone to school and graduated, and my grandchildren have grown up here, too. My wife, Phyllis, and I plant our garden and wait for the orioles and hummingbirds to return to our yard every Spring. She painted scenes of the four seasons on the living room walls of the 1835 house where we have lived for many decades, and that house is full of memories, friends, and music. Sometimes we hear distant voices singing even in the stillness of the night. Every day of the year I walk my dogs at dawn up and down the streets where friends and neighbors still keep faith with each other. Railroad tracks run right along this majestic river, and from our house we can hear the sound of the old steam train that carries passengers to the riverboat docked next to the town landing, where craftsmen once built ships to sail the Atlantic, and where steamers stopped to pick up passengers and cargo heading to New York. We listen for the clink of horseshoes on the green across from the Historical Society's old "Stone House" to mark the beginning of summer, and we gather at dusk on those warm nights to listen to local bands play into the night, and some of us get up and dance. We smile as the maples along our winding roads turn crimson in the fall, and we head to the white clapboard Congregational Church on Christmas Eve where the town's children act out the old Nativity story as many of their parents did once upon a time.

Changes have come, as they do everywhere. However, there is also a constancy about the succession of seasons and years. And the sorrows and dreams that fill our days and nights remind us that we are kindred in bone and blood, in soul and heart. Our river reminds us of the old hymn which refers to time as an "ever-rolling stream" that bears us all away in the end. But as its waters surge toward the great silver sea, we are also reminded that the flow of our time can be beautiful. And so it is necessary, always, to pay attention to the sweep of time and stars, and to notice in the midst of us the stories, miracles, and graces that make our lives rich, bright, sweet, holy.

So here is a year of watching my life in this lovely place. And in a poem for each of the 52 weeks (plus one), I offer my thanks for the life I have been given. I hope it reminds you of the life you have been given, too.

January

January

Sparrows' New Year

Today is a new year. For us, the passage of time is momentous. We face this passage with some bravery, because it makes us remember that our stock of these things is running low. None of us gets too many years to spend. So we plow into the year with a certain intention to make things better while we have a chance. We vow to lose weight or exercise more. We intend to be more tolerant of the foolishness and flaws of others, and if we are wise, we hope to be more forgiving to ourselves.

Years ago, Phyllis and I planned a wonderful New Year's Eve. It was a major turning of the calendar, the edge of a century beginning with the number 20. Some looked at the coming of year "Y2K" as ominous. Prophets of doom said that computers would fail all over the world. One man warned me that our church should be stockpiling food, water, guns and money to prepare for the catastrophe that was sure to come (it was in the Bible, you know). Phyllis and I had other plans. We put on our fanciest clothes—a gown and a tuxedo—and headed off to an elegant party, in spite of the fact that we were both recuperating from a terrible case of the flu. We could hardly stand up as we sipped champagne, and finally we excused ourselves from dinner well before 10 p.m. and made our way home. We fell into bed, turned on the TV, watched reruns of the fireworks over the Eiffel

Tower, and fell asleep. We did not make it to midnight in Connecticut, but we woke up the next day and the world was still here.

So today, we begin the great wheel of the year again. The world is still here. I am too, for the time being. I celebrate that I am not alone. And I have faith that is good to begin again.

Sparrows' New Year

The sparrows huddle in the forsythia
this cold, cold morning,
a choir waiting for the altos to show up,
and with no particular song in mind.
I would teach them
a chorus of Auld Lang Syne,
remind them of a day, once,
when the world was young,
and love was sweet.
I would teach them, too,
to make some plans,
to dream of some better idea than this,
perhaps a sparrow heaven.
But for them, this day is young,
and love is as sweet as a winter sun on feathers
and a morning full of seeds.
Like today, for them
every day is a beginning,
a new year,
a good place to hold on,
where they can move closer together
when the night comes.

January

Cold

Yesterday was almost as cold as it gets here in Connecticut in the winter. The Great Plains have been assailed by the same "polar vortex," which makes it dangerous just to be alive and outdoors at the same time. I think about the wild creatures seeking some shelter from the wind, perhaps finding some little warmth in each other to help them survive. We do not belong in such weather. We hide in our little homes, relying on the hum of furnaces and the sagging wires that carry electric current from pole to pole through the brutal arctic cold. We forget how close we are to perishing.

I remember the winter of my senior year at a college in Minnesota, which was perched on a hilltop where the wind raged in below zero temperatures. My old red Ford sedan spent these winter nights in a flat, exposed parking lot. For many nights in that most bitterly cold January term I would set my alarm and get up at 2 or 3 in the morning and drive around that little town just so that I could keep that car from freezing over altogether. Eventually I got the bright idea of disconnecting the battery and bringing it into the dormitory where it spent the night under my bed. That nice warm battery would be all set to turn over that frozen motor in the morning.

But the true measure of cold, for me, was when, as a boy, I would be outside, playing in the snow until there was no feeling left in my mittened hands. I would head inside, toss my mittens on the radiator, and run hot water over my hands. I could barely stand it. Those cold fingers would ache as the warmth worked its way down toward the bone, then sting as the blood would begin to circulate again. The windows would be rattling, etched with frost, but my hands around a cup of hot chocolate made the world all right. This is winter's gift, that we sometimes have the power to make the world habitable for each other in the most intolerable of times.

Cold

This cold rules over a world
not fit for us.
It bites deep, stings,
hurries us to a place of shelter.
Overhead the trees cry out,
great limbs creaking in the night,
keeping the squirrels awake,
curled up in their open holes
and dreaming of spring.
All are strangers here,
in this alien world
stripped to the bone.
A kind of hunger rises in us,
a longing for another season
that feels more like home.
But here, in this winter exile,
we know the truth:
that we must make our own shelter
to rest, to endure, to grow.
Sometimes it is enough
to warm each others' hands,

to pull the blankets round,
and then to wait
for something inside us
to burn again.

January

The Empty Chairs

This week we have enjoyed a January thaw here in Connecticut. The snow is almost gone, except on the edges of streets and parking lots where it had been plowed into piles not too long ago. There has been a softness in the air, and we have been able to walk outside just a little slower now that the bitter arctic cold has left us for a while. The old New England farmers never relaxed on a nice day, of course. They learned to expect that storm and troubles were always just around the corner, and that it was a good idea to prepare yourself for them.

But I am not an old Yankee farmer. I will take these days with gratitude, even though I know that there is a lot more of winter yet to come. So I wander through my back yard, and up into the woods, where the bare bones of the landscape show themselves most clearly in winter. And walking back toward the house I notice that the melting snow has revealed again all the tasks which were unfinished last fall. The yard is covered with wet, matted leaves that I never got around to raking up. The garden is a mess of skeletal flower and vegetable stalks. Over in one corner a covey of plastic pink flamingos lean against the fence, and the pole of prayer flags that wave brightly in the wind on a spring day has drooped into the mud. A gazing ball over by the barn is off its perch, nestled in the stubble underneath the lilacs.

And up by the terrace, where the yard backs up to the woods, are two metal chairs that threaten to be obscured by overgrown forsythia. Nobody has sat in them, probably for years. They are rusty and need paint, but they sit there, together, like an old married couple looking out over the debris and remnants of their lives. From this vantage point, I look down a gentle hill toward the house and garden, and beyond the fence and across the street to the white Congregational Church. I can remember, from here, my now grown-up children playing wiffle ball and hide-and-seek, and I can see other faces, some long gone, looking at the world from this very place. I can see myself here, too, all of those years—a life passing in this same metal chair. And I wonder, too, who will sit in the empty chairs of my life in whatever years remain.

The Empty Chairs

The chairs are empty
out there near the edge of the woods,
under the bare trees
which give no shade
from winter's spare and fractious light.
I should have dragged them away,
warehoused them for a season
in the dusty barn loft
or in a basement corner
where they would sit in the dark
waiting for the grass to green again.
But I like them there, among the wet leaves,
rusted and empty.
Ghosts of the past sit there,
and I wait, and wonder,
about who may yet come
into this yard, this life,
to fill these empty spaces.
It is not a good place to sit, now,
even in this January thaw
which has exposed the unkempt garden,
the broken remnants of marigolds
and sunflower heads, hanging limply,

colorless as the cold earth.
Once my father sat here, though,
looking out at the climbing peas
and beyond, to the roses,
as a white cloud bloomed overhead
in the bluest sky.

January

The Zen of Cats

It snowed again last night, and this morning required boots and gloves and shovels. And, of course, time to go outside and make it passable for us who must get back into the world again. Inside the warm house, afterwards, there was waiting for me hot coffee and a crossword puzzle, and Ming, one of our two Siamese cats. He loves to jump up onto the table, square in the middle of the open newspaper, and rub against me until I offer a luxurious massage of his ears and belly.

Ming is the darker of the two cats we rescued from an animal shelter several years ago. We went there with the idea of possibly adopting one Siamese cat, but the shelter supervisor confessed that there were actually two of them that had come in together. "It would be a shame to split them up," he added, "though of course you could just take the one if you want." Of course, we came home with two. Sushi, the more timid of the two, hid out around the house for over a year, coming out only at night to eat. I thought for a while she had slipped out the back door when it had been left ajar. Ming has always been more social, and he always seeks out my attention when I am trying to do something else.

Yet these cats bring a certain Zen-like presence into the home. Often I find them sharing a sunspot on the living room floor, or curled up together on the warm cable TV box, or purring in stereo as they languorously lay braided together on top of the radiator while the snow flies outside. I have heard it said that cats are mysterious and spiritual creatures who may, from time to time, leave their bodies via astral projection while they seem to be sleeping. I think it's more likely that they just know how to be content in the present moment. No worries, no plans, no fears. Just this moment to be warm.

The Zen of Cats

They seek some warm place,
perhaps just a small halo of sun
to be their simple solace.
Entwined, they are one,
comforted by each other's
familiar deep-throated rumble.
They are centered, serene,
content to be creatures
who have found their place,
even as the world goes off to work,
or worries itself to wakefulness,
or scours the pestilent streets
for food and kindness,
or waits for love to warm it through.
This is what I wish
sometimes:
to stretch out, silent enough
to hear my own heart,
to be warm inside for a while,
and, like a cat,
to just be.

January

Seeds

The past few weeks have been a harsh January cold spell, but the days are getting a bit longer and the seed catalogs have been enticing me with their usual bounty of optimism. Someone once said that January is the best month for beans, because it's the time we dream of next year's garden. And we imagine that garden in the pictures of the catalogs, free of sweat and bugs and dry spells that will inevitably discourage us come July. I love to look at the front section of all those catalogs, which are full of the best new varieties of vegetables and flowers for the coming year. This year's crop of offerings includes such wonders as a heart-shaped, rose-colored tomato; a golden snow pea; and a cute little climbing cucumber. How can I resist ordering a new pink rose called "Jump for Joy" that smells like apples?

And now my seed orders have begun to arrive. Of course, it's still too early for me to sow them. Sometime late next month I will begin to plant, starting my seeds in small boxes of potting soil which I will gently water, wrap in plastic, and place on top of the furnace until they germinate. Then the flats will go under lights on a table in the basement, and passers-by peeking in the cellar windows will wonder what it is that's growing tall and green down there.

But, for now, I shake the packets and look at the pictures in the catalogs and dream of the heady scent of great purple lilacs and the taste of the first peas snapped from the vines in the sweet days when apple blossoms fly and the earth smells rich and wet and good. And I remember that all of the best things in our lives start as seeds waiting to sprout and grow. Sometimes they don't seem to amount to much—our little loves, our little efforts to be good and true and honorable. But it's a good thing to hold on to them anyway, especially in January.

Seeds

In my hands
I hold hope.
In these bitter days
the wind laughs,
stings, until eyes water,
and fingers, numb,
reach for an envelope
bearing promise.
Here are Matt's Wild Cherry Tomatoes,
Orange Sun Peppers,
and Carnival Hollyhocks.
And someday, soon,
I will spill dirt into trays,
and sprinkle these seeds
into the fertile darkness
and watch for green.
It is enough, now, to wait,
to dream of purple and red
where all is white, barren,
to know that every good thing—
courage, wonder, glory, love—
has its January
where there are only seeds
in our trembling hands.

February

February

February, Stillness

Sunday was Groundhog Day, and here it was overcast for a while before the sun broke out. Traditionalists interpreted that to mean that winter will endure a while longer. But I don't need a groundhog to know that. Winter hangs on in New England, with fits and starts, through February and March until some soft and unexpected day when the skunk cabbage push up through the mud and the peepers start their night song. But we are a long way from that.

We awoke to another winter storm this morning—the second this week. There is a certain resignation that seems to take over at this point. The school district didn't even decide to wait and see how this one might turn out. They called off today's school sessions yesterday while the sun was bright and warm. And this morning the streets were completely quiet. Not even the usual snowplows had begun the task of clearing the roads.

So my morning routine of walking the dogs at dawn became a surreal adventure into the mystery of winter. Slogging through the deepening snow, we had to make our own path through an unbroken expanse of white, which seemed to be under, around, and over us all at once. And then I became aware of the silence, and the fact that there was no wind at all. This gift will not last. But, for the moment, the stillness settled softly, like snow gathering on shoulders.

February, Stillness

The wind chimes hang still
unmoved by the breaking light
or the cascade of snow
filling the earth.
Winter often prowls like a beast
slinking through stones and bushes
and lurking around forbidding corners,
its breath icy with the otherness
of sea and stars.
I walk north, feel the sting and bite,
then finally turn my face homeward,
my back to the wind,
pushed on by its force
hard against my legs and heart.
But then a morning comes
still and silent, breathless,
and wonder, too, and gratitude,
that for a while this winter morning
is pregnant, waiting for something—
a different breath, perhaps—
to stir again,
like a song.

February

Love

It is two days until Valentine's Day, and we will be braving the winter weather to go to a party at a lovely old house on the Connecticut shoreline. I will be wearing the tuxedo we found at a consignment shop several years ago. It happened to be just my size, but even at that I was reluctant to purchase it. "When will I ever need to wear a tuxedo?" I asked. Well, as it turns out, on Valentine's Day this year, and any number of other occasions where it is just fun to get all dressed up and remember how lovely life can be. I even learned how to tie a bow tie (no clip-ons for me anymore) and I ordered a beautiful, big red patterned crimson tie for this occasion.

We need such graciousness in our lives from time to time. It seems especially fitting that Valentine's Day falls in the middle of February, when it feels like this season of cold and snow will never end. We are imprisoned in gray and dirty white, stone and cold, and, at the same time, by the awareness of how cold and lonely our world can be. So the legend of the original Saint Valentine emerges from a prison, too. Nobody is sure who the real Saint Valentine was. Some say he was an early Christian martyr who died in prison for his faith, but not before he cured the jailer's blind daughter and left her a loving note signed, "Your Valentine." Relics of his body are all over the world. His bones are claimed by churches in Poland

and Italy, France and the Czech Republic, in Dublin, Ireland, and even somewhere in Missouri. But the truth is that all these centuries later, he belongs to all of us.

We nod to him with gratitude this Friday, send cards and flowers and chocolate, and wear tuxedos and red bow ties to parties. We write our notes from the prison of this continuing winter because if it all ended right here, right now, the only thing we'd want to leave behind as a token for people to remember us is our love.

Love

Sometimes love is light
as a leaf carried by a breath of wind
to dance across the snow,
a remnant from the heart
of tree, of earth, of sun—
this lovely sigh of a thing,
that makes everything more lovely.
Sometimes love is heavy
as stone
enough to break the heart
of tree, of earth, of sun,
a borne burden, an ache,
a song that keens at death, or loss,
a lever to move a mountain.
We shall find this love,
we shall.
It is what makes life,
and breaks it,
the thing we must find or die.
We would do anything for it.
We carry it into the darkness,

into the fire, the flood,
into death, to nothingness,
or perhaps, to the dancing place.
Mostly, it carries us.

February

Ice

February is the shortest month in days, but it feels so long. Everywhere the piles of frozen slush and snow have grown higher and higher, and people are weary of winter. Perhaps it is because it is both cold and colorless, and because—if there are portents of Spring around us—they cannot yet be seen. It will take a good melt, but then the little snowdrops will rise from the detritus of winter, and soon after that the purple crocus will push into view, and it will be time to cut the pussy willows.

For now, we remember that this is winter's last hurrah. And what a hurrah it has been. Snowfall after snowfall, and icicles hanging from the eaves, and deep paths out to the birdfeeders, and treacherous walks where the snow has melted and frozen and melted and frozen again. After last Saturday's snow, I grabbed a shovel and headed out to the driveway to clear the car. I have warned Phyllis many times about the step at the corner of the barn which catch the drips from the corner of the roof—the "widow maker," I call it. This time, I forgot. My feet went flying out in front of me and as I saw the pattern of branches directly over my head, I felt the ensuing fall happen in almost slow motion. I remember thinking to myself, "This is not good. This will not end well."

It did not end well, though not as badly as it might have. There were no broken bones, no blood. I landed on the back pocket of my jeans, right where I carry my cell phone. As I lay on the ice, I fished out the cracked phone which was of no use to call for help, if I had needed to. Only later, in the house, could I admire the large purple bruise spreading over my backside. Yesterday it started snowing again. I wait for pussy willows.

Ice

This crystal, bright-shining thing
diamond-hard, alive,
builds its beautiful prison
on stem and leaf,
glitters hard on earth
that would wish to soften, breathe,
wear some greener garment.
Long shards dangle from the edges
of our sheltered world,
say, "Beware,
you who step
into this bitter loveliness."
Who would choose glitter
instead of grace?
So we should be wary
of all cold and callous glory,
seek instead a tender way to be,
easily bruised, or broken,
yet alive,
a leaf in waiting,
a sign of Spring.

February

Blue Irises

When I woke up yesterday morning, the dream was still fresh. I carried it with me into the day, and even now the memory of it lingers. Perhaps it is the color of the irises, blue as a late spring morning, that filled my waking vision. They were everywhere, in bunches and mounds, surrounding a friend who was suffering a grave illness. The illness was there, too, in my dream, perhaps an illness unto death. But those glorious blue flowers seem to be a sign of some hopefulness, some beatific presence in the midst of the doom.

Something like this happens every year, in late winter. These frigid, colorless days, end on end, create a kind of sensory deprivation. I begin dreaming in technicolor. Even awake, I imagine the world in hues of May: great clusters of purple lilacs filling the air with their heady scent; huge peonies unfolding, glowing pink in morning light; golden sundrops waving in the breeze; and the unmatchable blue of those Siberian irises. I could swim in it. Perhaps the thing I feel is the allure of life itself, poised and prepared to erupt someday, but for the moment invisible beneath the layers of granular ice and grit that still cover our landscape.

At the end of the day yesterday, I came home and smiled at the oil painting hanging in our front hall, an image of an old Midwestern farmer standing in a bed of irises, his house a faint dream of a thing behind him. It was painted by a west coast artist, Marilyn Lowe, and entitled "Another Spring." There is a sadness in the farmer's face, and I wonder if it is because he is alone amid such beauty. Or perhaps the house in the background is his dream—a yearning for home, for a place of belonging, an assurance that love is just as real as those blue irises.

Blue Irises

Hungry for warmth, for life,
I dream color
into this barren season
which is bereft of it.
Here and there
the snow pulls back
from the edges of roads,
and something resembling green
hints at life.
I look hard, wait for a brave
green tip or bud to appear.
I lean toward Spring.
And at the edges of sorrow,
amid the dull weariness of pain
or regret,
I try to remember
a day of irises,
a glorious tapestry in blue,
bright as heaven,
and hope a little.

March

March

Ash Wednesday

There was shrimp etoufee to eat and lots of New Orleans style music at the Mardi Gras party last night at our town's senior center. It was probably a little different from what took place on Bourbon Street. There were feathers and beads and masks, even a palm reader in the corner. A few folks, trying to converse at their tables, asked that the music be turned down a little. After the meal, some of the seniors got up, drawn by the lively music, and dodged the metal walkers as they danced. The party ended early.

Mardi Gras is the celebration of carnival, which means "farewell to the flesh." It is a reminder of the ancient Lenten tradition of fasting from meat, but it could just as well be a warning of our own earthly limits. Perhaps the wild exuberance of Rio or New Orleans pales a bit as we get older, and that's why last night's partiers went to bed early. As we age, we get closer to our own "farewell to the flesh." It is not a bad thing, of course, to be reminded of our mortality. The hope is that we savor the days that are given to us. We should live them all as gifts.

This morning I went outside early to fill the bird feeders. I found our little pond had been desecrated during the night, the pump knocked over, the water murky, the goldfish gone. A trail of blood and scales led off across the crust of snow, and we guessed that a hungry raccoon had made a nocturnal visit. It was just a few fish, I told myself, even though I have fed those fish for several summers and winters. I knew their markings, sometimes called them by name. And so I am sad for the loss of my scaled brothers and sisters. And I am stung by the reminder that all of us are just dust and ashes, who are facing the party's end. Carpe diem.

Ash Wednesday

The brown earth begins to show,
taking sun,
so that life can happen again.
We are drawn to this ancient awakening,
drawn to some pulse in dirt and stone
that is our own.
So we come to a moment
of dust and ashes
to remember what is in us.
We step away from our days of dancing,
the wild carnival of pretending
that we are young, that laughter is forever,
and that singing hearts may drown out
the wails of grief, or the silent desolations
of our waiting loneliness.
We come from the wishful feast
still hungry for love's banquet,
still waiting for a better season,
for something simple in us,
like loam or humus,
which is ready to take sun.

March

Signs

Walking through the center of town early this morning, I barely noticed them at first. There were blackbirds high up in the trees, flapping their wings and moving from branch to branch in the gathering daylight. Ten minutes later and a few blocks away, they were still up above me. I once knew a man who believed that a flock of crows followed him around, even as he moved from place to place, city to city. There is either a certain aura of paranoia about the suspicion that we are being followed—or an overdeveloped sense of our importance in the cosmic order that makes us think that even the birds are interested in what we are doing.

When I got home, I was settled in to reading the morning paper and having my coffee when my wife called me to the back door. She smiled as we stepped outside, and pointed to the tall maple in the side yard, where a large cloud of male red-wing blackbirds had taken roost, their spring song filling the morning. They were back! The red-wings' arrival is one of the surest signs of the changing season, their unmistakable trill and distinctive "conk-a-reeeee" proclaiming, "It's Spring!" Soon the females will arrive, too, and the marshes will be busy with nesting. The hills and yards are still a mess of gritty snow, but for now, I have my oracle. Today or tomorrow I will take a walk through the mushy snow that fills the woods, and I will hunt for the first striped points of skunk cabbage rising from the mud. I may find, along the way, a few snowdrops taking the sun in a sheltered place, or see an early bee hungry for a crocus. I even will be glad if a few blackbirds are interested enough to follow me.

Signs

You have to know
what to look for.
Spring is not first announced
by waves of daffodils
or the eruption of blossoms
on the wild forsythia.
Go among the sodden leaves,
and look for a stretch of mud
where a skunk cabbage peeks out,
oblivious of cold,
or watch for a haze of red
on the face of a distant hill,
or notice a sealed willow bud
split into a silver smile,
or listen for a song in the morning
as a dark visitor flashes its wings
in flight,
a crimson badge of joy.

March

St. Joseph's Day

Today is St. Joseph's Day, most notably the time when the swallows return to the old mission in San Juan Capistrano, California. But I remember this day every year for another reason. It is Irene's birthday. For many years she and her husband operated the little bakery on Main Street, getting up in the dark of the night to make the breads, cakes and rolls that would fill the glass cases and welcome morning visitors. The cinnamon buns were my favorite, and maybe the dark, sweet molasses bread for which they were famous. But the real joy was Irene's welcome, in her strong German accent, as she offered a "Good morning, sweetheart!" or "How are you, darling?" as I walked through the door, then slipped an extra roll into the bag. March 19 was Irene's birthday, and every year I would bring her a bouquet of daffodils to thank her for being a gracious part of my life.

The bakery has been gone for many years. But March 19 still pops up in my mental calendar: Irene's birthday. The year unravels that way. Not just a succession of numerical dates, but a tapestry of memories that mark the important moments of our lives. For me, this week not only significant for Irene's birthday. Monday, St. Patrick's Day, was the anniversary of the day that our son suffered a severe brain injury that left him hospitalized and recovering for over a year. Thursday is the Spring Equinox, when I look forward to having flats of seeds sprouting in anticipation of this summer's garden. Friday is the annual Volunteer Fire Department banquet, on a night which sometimes ends with the joyful nighttime song of the spring peepers.

These occasions will not be marked in newspapers or history books, but they are every bit as important to me as the headline events of our time. They mark the people and experiences that have shaped me, the simple gifts which have given me joy, the challenges that have stretched me and helped me grow. They make me stop in time, to remember, and to be grateful for all the holy days I celebrate. Today I will get a bunch of daffodils, and give thanks for Irene.

St. Joseph's Day

Today the swallows return
to the old California mission,
and Spring will be here again.
One curious legend claims
that the birds fly thousands of miles—
all the way from Jerusalem—
carrying twigs which can float,
so that they can perch on them
and rest during their long journey.
Perhaps we are sojourners, too,
and the twigs we carry
are the memories
of those who have peopled our lives,
and the dark and sweet passages
that have sustained us on the way.
I gather a bunch of bright daffodils
to remember this day,
to honor one good and shining face
who smiles in my gallery of grace
as spring comes again.

March

Holy Ground

He leaned forward in his wheelchair, his eyes hidden behind an enormous pair of sunglasses as a protection from the bright sunlight streaming through the window. So I could not see the grimace, or the tears, as he told me the story of their life together of over sixty years. They had met once upon a time at a silver factory where she worked, and where he drove a delivery truck. From the first he had loved her, had set his sights on marriage.

On the wall was a photo of their wedding, she in her long white gown, he in a suit that seemed like an extravagance—something awkward and out of the ordinary for him. We do things like that—the fancy clothes, the flowers—out of sheer love. And that is what it was, all those years, Art and Jean, husband and wife. "Wasn't she beautiful," he said. I turned to see her twisted on an institutional bed, her eyes squeezed shut, her mouth open, trying to die. She could not answer now, could not tell her version of the story of this life. "Yesterday," he said, "I woke up in the night because I heard her calling me: Artie! Artie!" The nurse's aide had come to him, helped him up from the wheelchair, held him by the waist as he leaned as far over the bed as he could reach—far enough to press his lips on hers, to answer her cry in the night with one last kiss.

Before I left Art there, in the room beside his dying wife, he shared a last confession. "You know she was married before— when she was very young. He went over to fight in the war, and died in the Battle of the Bulge. She never saw him again." He paused, swallowed hard. "And now she'll be back with him." I took his hand, and we sat in silence for a moment, balancing in the space between us the weight of sixty years as a fragile treasure.

Holy Ground

We should not see some things, perhaps:
the stranger's tears that flow
in some unguarded moment
when joy or loss or hurt
rips open the silent heart;
the most private touch
of hand to face of lovers
in their delicious, tender darkness;
a mother grasping a child
in their first or last parting.
These things happen on holy ground,
bidding us to silence, or awe.
So when this once most eager groom
bends to kiss his aged, broken bride—
still in his fading eyes
the most beautiful of mortal souls—
I turn away.
And this I know:
If she should die in this one moment,
it would be love itself that wraps
them both around,
filling this antiseptic room
with some wild incense—hyacinth or sweetest rose—

and I would have to bend in reverence,
remove my shoes,
and thank the sun and stars
that this old world may wear us down
and tear our hearts apart,
yet also give us this.

March

Peepers and Peas

Last night we heard them. In one of those marshy areas where life first rises every Spring, the peepers were singing their tiny hearts out. Here in New England, the annual appearance of Hyla crucifer is one of the surest signs that Spring has come. These little tree frogs climb out of the muck of their winter habitation and begin their ceremony of love. They are hard to see, but when you find one, you will know it by the cross streaked across its back (hence the species name crucifer). In high churches, the crucifer is the person who begins the mass by carrying the cross down the center aisle into the chancel. In the cathedral of nature, little Hyla crucifer begins the celebration, too, carrying its cross into Spring's moonlight while filling the night with its song.

There are other signs of Spring abounding now, too. Monday was the last day of March, and now we are just feeling April's gentle embrace. The pussy willows are in full tuft, soon to sport the golden pollen which will be carried away by the soft breezes of April. There are still snowbirds around, but fewer of them. The inexorable journey northward has begun. The allure of this season is in my blood. My great uncle Emil was a Midwestern bachelor farmer. He could read a change of weather by the feel of the air and the movement of the leaves in the trees, and his garden was planted by the phases of the moon. Peas were the first into the ground, always in the waxing moon before Easter. I never disputed this wisdom, because he could make anything grow. I grow a garden because of him, I think, but I make it a little simpler. I plant peas the last day of March.

A few weeks ago the prospects of a March planting was not hopeful. Snow covered the garden, and the sod underneath felt pretty hard. But this is the miracle, the one that the peepers feel deep in the mud of their cold ponds. The sun gives life, even when we don't see that it is happening. March 31 dawned cold and raw, and soon ice and sleet was falling upon us. But by afternoon it was done, and the sun peered out. At five o'clock my wife and I stepped into our bedraggled remnant of a garden, turned the earth and crumbled a handful to see if it was dry enough, then raked an area clear enough to press wrinkled seeds of Cascadia peas into the dirt. I wanted to sing like a peeper.

Peepers and Peas

Such a sound!
High and shrill,
their voices fill the night,
and we pause in the darkness
surrounded by Spring,
senses keen to the scent of awakening.
We are held by this mystery,
the surge of life,
the turning of a clock
that is deep inside the world.
I gather a handful of wrinkled seeds,
press them into the moist earth
and give them to the darkness and light
with a wordless blessing,
believing that they, too,
understand the wild song of peepers
and know that something holy,
like love,
is stirring them to life.

April

April

Wren's Song

The little wren is singing its heart out again. It has been a long winter, but yesterday the air was soft and the rain didn't seem to cast a pall over the day at all. Late in the afternoon the sun smiled from the breaking clouds, and it was a time to just stand and wonder at the age-old miracle happening around us. "Now the green blade riseth," the French carol proclaims. And a day of Spring rain seems to green the earth right before our eyes. Over on Elm Street, a yard is filled with the blue of Siberian squill rising from the winter-weathered grass. But there is nothing as full of Spring's joy as the song of the Carolina wren on a tender afternoon. The bird books say that the song of this wren sounds something like "teakettle, teakettle, teakettle!" Perhaps so. And this seems appropriate for this little creature who inhabits the edges of a world that feels like we are home at last.

We all have a place that makes our heart sing. This morning my wife left before dawn to visit a hospital and orphanage in Port-au-Prince, Haiti. She has made that trip a number of times since the catastrophic earthquake there in 2010. She felt a tug at her heart then to go and offer her nursing skills, mostly in community health clinics in the devastated neighborhoods where cholera was epidemic. What she found amid the broken buildings and impossible streets was people with amazing spirit and even joy, and they have taken up residence inside of her. These past weeks she has been collecting baby clothes, lotion, diaper cream, and other supplies to distribute to new mothers who sometimes have nothing to offer their babies except love. She may also visit the city morgue with Father Rick Frechette of St. Damien Hospital as he goes to offer a dignified and loving burial to bodies that have remained there unclaimed.

On the counter in the kitchen Phyllis' datebook lay open to a page where she had stuck a small handwritten note from our granddaughter. "Dear Mimi," it said. "I love you so much I can't wate [sic] to spend the night at your house." That's how Phyllis feels about going to Haiti. Maybe that's how that wren feels out behind the barn, singing Spring into being. "Teakettle, teakettle, teakettle!"

Wren's Song

Over the just-turned earth,
up into the budded branches
of great trees swaying in an April breeze,
through the glass of a kitchen window
shining with afternoon light,
the song soars,
a mighty thing from a tiny heart.
It is an endless emanation of joy,
as if this melody has been bottled up
too long,
and now flows as wild and free
as Spring and love,
as if the canticle itself had wings and feathers
and must take flight.
Perhaps we all are wrens,
and every sullen creature—
every humble, wintered one of us—
has something burning deep inside,
a fire, a joy, a love, a song,
and we will not live,
nor will Springtime ever fully come,
until we dare to sing.

April

Sun Dog

Fifty years ago one of the most powerful earthquakes in modern history resulted from a rupture in a fault running under Prince William Sound off the coast of Alaska. It was Good Friday, and when the earth roared and rumbled, collapsing buildings and roads and sending enormous tidal waves throughout the Pacific, there were those who believed that the apocalypse had surely come. They were reminded of another earthquake that shook the earth during a terrible crucifixion centuries ago. Omens in the earth and sky have been forever with us. A comet flashed across the sky after the assassination of Julius Caesar in 44 BC, and William the Conqueror believed that the appearance of Halley's Comet in 1066 was a sign that the Norman invasion of Britain would be successful. Eclipses, too, have marked great historic events, like the lunar eclipse that presaged the fall of Constantinople in 1453 after over 1,000 years as a center of politics and culture.

This week across North America a full lunar eclipse has been the first of four "blood moons" that will visit the skies between now and September of next year. These eclipses are called "blood moons" because the moon turns a reddish color as it passes into earth's shadow. At least one conservative preacher is getting some publicity by predicting that this is our sign that the world as we know it is about to come to an end. But the truth is that the world as we know it is always coming to an end. Countries change governments and cultural norms shift as we sleep. Our beloved time will come to an end, and we will, too.

And outside, the grass pushes up from the barren ground and another winter of our life is gone. Yesterday we sat outside in the April afternoon and watched a hawk circle overhead. Big yellowed heads of pussy willow dropped to the greening earth as the breeze stirred their branches. Up on the edge of the terrace I noticed a sapling that was nearly eight feet high. Where did that come from, and how had I not noticed it before? Clouds drifted overhead, and suddenly a beautiful sundog glimmered through the tree branches. This bright bit of rainbow light is a sign, too. Like the great earthquakes, our little sundog appeared during Holy Week. Maybe it is reminding me that something holy is going on even in the crux of change. I think that is true. Rain is coming, the sundog promises. That is good news for the peas and lettuce newly planted in the garden, and I think it is good news for all of us who wait expectantly for a new day.

Sun Dog

The world is free-falling, broken-winged,
flailing in a crosswind
that bends trees, shakes earth,
turns the taciturn moon to look away.
So, afraid of what we cannot see,
we hold on to little things,
pretend our permanence.
We work the morning puzzle,
take a walk, do laundry, eat an orange.
We look out the window at Spring.
Today the dog lies in the new grass,
smells the change in the air,
rolls so that the sun can warm her underside,
sleeps as if all were well.
We wish it so,
and feel the flame of sun
in the free-fall of the world,
scatter tiny seeds into broken earth
in case the rain comes,
and look up as a piece of rainbow
suddenly smiles at the edge
of this frail day.

April

Easter Hands

Today, April 23, is William Shakespeare's birthday, a date kept by convention because nobody knows exactly when he was born. He died on April 23, too, an odd fact that I learned in high school English literature class—one of those peculiar things that takes up residence in your head even though it's hard to work into conversations at dinner parties. However, we should give thanks for Shakespeare, and for his signature written across all of Western culture. He gave us the glory of words, and the glory of an imagination that captures the very essence of humanity—its heights and its depths—in poems and plays that shall endure to the end of civilization. Today, to honor his legacy, I am going down to the steps of our Town Hall and read all 154 of his sonnets, a manageable feat compared to reading all the plays.

Still, I hope that my voice holds out. This body of flesh, like all humans', will give out long before the words of Shakespeare. And here, in these sweet days of April, I want to sing a "Hey nonino" like the Bard's lover and lass walking across Spring's green fields. Because in the passage of years, the days become all the more precious. They are to be held, cherished, sung. Shakespeare reminds us that soon this abounding life will fade, giving way to autumn's "bare ruined choirs" and the twilight years of "death's second self." So, he concludes,

"This thou perceivest, which makes thy love more strong,
To love that well which thou must leave ere long."

And we do feel this love, and every Spring its power seems to grow more strong as our time on this tender planet ticks away.

Last week I visited an elderly acquaintance whose remaining Aprils are numbered. She greeted me with joy and a contagious laugh, and held out her aging hands to display an array of artwork on her fingernails. "Look at my nails," she beamed. "For Easter!" They were pastels, pink and yellow and blue, and two were decorated with rabbits. We laughed together, glad that some joys are ageless. There is still a fire in us, old and young. It is sometimes banked in the corner's of our soul's hearth, coals gone cold from neglect, or from the long accumulation of sorrows. But the embers burn and wait for a breath to raise them to life. A few daffodils may do it, or the smell of rain, or sunlight on the river, or the violets erupting in a barren meadow. Or, who knows, some love may yet smile through those bare ruined choirs, fill our hearts, make us paint our nails and read some Shakespeare on April 23. Hey ding a ding, ding!

Easter Hands

I would hold this day,
tight in my aching grasp,
made weaker by the unfeeling years
as they wear this body toward dust.
I would hold this Spring in Easter hands,
sink them deep into the turned earth,
run these fingers through long grass,
raise them to catch the sky,
or hold in them some wondrous seed
where life is hidden away,
a sentient spirit caught until the dark
enfolds it, and then the rain
calls it to find its morning.
I would hold today in Easter hands,
until the bones and flesh go limp at last,
and then I would give back
the wonders that they always held,
give them again to the spring
where lovers come to drink,
give back the joy, the fire,
give back the golden blossom
of this one and treasured life.

April

May Day

There is no green like the color in a late April day. Today a line of willows shines in the afternoon light, a neon green with golden highlights. It is what I call Easter green, and it is also erupting in the tiny flowers on a thousand maple trees and in the new foliage on the lilacs waving in the breeze next to the barn. And on the hillside, close to the ground beneath the canopy of trees, that same bright green makes even the hated Japanese barberry look beautiful. Amid this profusion of green, the bright yellow blooms of forsythia and daffodils and the deep purple of periwinkle and the profusion of violets in the meadow add to the breathtaking loveliness of these days. Even when it rains, the earth seems to smile.

Tomorrow is May Day. For millennia, this was a day to celebrate the return of life, and it was marked by a variety of celebrations that may or may not have been fertility rites. My grandmother recalled a tradition of her youth, when young people would gather flowers into May baskets, often made out of paper cones, then leave them on the doorstep of a beloved, bang on the door or ring the bell and run like the wind. If you were caught, it was forever. And then there was the ritual of a Maypole, to which long ribbons were attached. As I recall it, the point was that each young man took a ribbon and danced one direction, and the ladies went the other way, weaving in and out until the ribbons were all wound tight against the pole. In the end, you could wind up face to face with your one true love!

One of the treasured pictures of my father's childhood has him amid a group of friends, a tall Maypole in the background. He sits in the front row, finger up his nose. Romance apparently was not on his mind. Freud thought the Maypole was a phallic symbol; others weren't so sure. One idea was that the Maypole represented the "axis mundi," or the center axis of the world. And why not? We spin on this terrestrial ball, and at the center of everything is love's renewing power. More recently, May Day has been observed as International Workers' Day, and during the cold war years it was marked by parades of tanks and soldiers. I, for one, prefer the old version of the celebration. I like romance better than tanks. Yesterday I bent down to find a walnut amid the remnant of last fall's leaves, broken in two. Inside, a heart smiled. Happy May Day!

May Day

Sweet day,
gowned in green and gold,
you call us to dance with you
to an oriole's tune.
It is time for joy,
as ribbons of clouds fly
from the passing rain,
and the earth sings, sprouts,
rises true as a promise.
The living has been hard too long,
hard as a bitter hermit
red in hand from the cold
which gives no kindness.
And so the weary laborer,
who bends away from wind,
trusts no generous invitation
for fear that all true goods
are finally false,
and thus lives wretched
in a wounded world.
But some, instead, leave flowers at the door,
run to dance to the orioles' tune,
astonished at the secret

hidden in the hollow of this May day.
Here is a walnut split,
like the atoms of everything,
showing a heart,
and can it be that all is held together,
sings, sprouts, rises
out of love?

May

May

Bubble

These are sweet days, gentle, delicate. These May days are tender, as if their life is not quite fully formed. They are the times of birth and bud. Now the first life in the garden is apparent. The peas are an inch or two high, and the onion sets have pushed up through the friable earth with their tiny green swords. Soon it will be time for the first mowing of the grass, which is already dotted with golden blossoms of beautiful dandelions. Loveliest of all, I discovered this week that the Quaker Ladies are in bloom—waves and waves of them—in the vacant lots and across the cemetery's meadows, and even in the thin strips of earth between sidewalks and streets. Also known as bluets, these fragile little blossoms—blue with a golden center—are an ephemeral sign of Spring's promise.

Saturday, our granddaughters spent the day with us. The sun was shining, and a light breeze blew through the greening maple branches. It was a day for badminton and wiffle ball, for a hot dog picnic and a long ride on the swing. And for bubbles. It's never enough just to use the little soap bubble wand you can buy at the variety store. You need to pour quarts of the stuff into a upturned garbage can lid and use one of those big hoops that make enormous bubbles, bubbles with curious shapes and remarkable size, bubbles that rise and sail on the spring wind reflecting rainbows in their passage below the sun.

No matter how old you are, you want to have a turn at making bubbles like that. They make you laugh and cheer, marveling at their magic. There are laws of physics that explain a bubble, things that have to do with inner air pressure and surface tension. It is enough for me that they are wondrous and beautiful, and that anyone can make them. C.S. Lewis once wrote that love has three dimensions—one arising out of our needs, another from what we can give to others. The third is appreciative love, when we merely stand in awe, feeling joy or elation. Our heart wants to sing: "We give thee thanks for this great glory!" Sometimes we have this kind of love for what is holy. Sometimes we have it for bubbles, or Quaker Ladies winking at us in the grass.

Bubble

Up into the blue it sails,
shimmering with rainbow light,
held for a moment
on the wind—
an evanescent glory.
It is lifted by a breath,
and filled by a breath,
the very breath of one little life
that may be as ephemeral
as this bright thing.
We stand in a world
of passing wonders,
the choir of bluets on the cemetery hill,
the bee at rest on a quince blossom,
the wild mint rising in turned earth,
a child awake to joy,
and this sigh of delight in me,
this whisper of laughter
that slips out, rises like a bubble
full of breath,
and then is gone.

May
Lilacs

The hummingbirds are back, and the mosquitoes, too. This is truly the changing of seasons. I am ready to plant the tomato seedlings I have watched grow under the lights in my basement. My great uncle Emil knew that it was time to plant his fields—especially his sweet corn—when the leaves of the oak tree were the size of a squirrel's ear. For me, who does not climb up and measure the size of oak leaves, that is always around the middle of May, when the lilacs are in bloom. Right about now.

There was a time not too long ago when lilacs could be counted on blooming around Memorial Day. Children would gather the blossoms and lay them on the graves of fallen soldiers. In our day, they are mostly finished blooming by then. But now, in the middle of May, the great clusters of purple begin to open in the midday sun, their sweet aroma filling the air. In the bleak days of winter, I search the nursery catalogs for pictures of lilacs, and the anticipation of their wondrous blooms carries me through the colorless days.

There were lilacs a-plenty on our wedding day, 21 years ago tomorrow. My beloved and her sister went out the night before our marriage to gather lilac blooms along the country roads of Connecticut. The church and reception were decked with armfuls of those beautiful blossoms. I even wore a tie adorned with lilacs. Their blossoms still remind me of the sweetness of that day, filled with love's utter loveliness. Perhaps I am not the only one who cherishes these May beauties. Go out into the woods throughout New England, and soon enough you will come to a tall patch of lilacs. Perhaps there will be a clearing, and the lilacs will mark the place where once settlers planted a homestead. Nearby there likely will be the remnant of an old chimney, or the foundation of a little house where love tried to set roots and build a future. The lilacs still growing there are a sign that love will not give up.

Lilacs

Should this world of mine pass away,
this old house, solid and chimneyed,
the big barn, steady under the shade
of ancient maples,
the stone paths leading to the door—
should they one day sag
under the weight of time,
fall into themselves and slumber
under the tangles of bittersweet and ivy,
yet there shall be this:
one May morning the tall persistence
of lilacs
will yet rise into the sun and blue above,
and they will make purple clusters,
sweet as holy incense,
to hallow the day with a memory.
Perhaps someone will pass by,
see in the blooms some ancient gratitude,
and know that once a home was here,
know that once before the fall,
the sadness, the ache of parting,
there was a joy,
know that one spring day lilacs bloomed
at a most beautiful wedding.

May

Family Reunion

It was a joy to find, at the end of the driveway, a beautiful pile of manure—the gift of a friend with horses. When you have a garden, there is nothing sweeter than a load of manure. I was happily carting it into the garden to mix with the dirt under my tomato plants when a sparrow landed on a branch above me, long blades of grass in its beak. I paused to watch as she flew to the birdhouse on the side of the barn, disappeared inside, then popped out to repeat the process over and over again. There seemed to be two of them lining the nest with bits of leaf and grass, in anticipation of the brood which would soon emerge. I will never know the little sparrows-to-be with any intimacy, but somehow they have already become a part of my family.

This Saturday my wife's family will hold its annual reunion in our back yard here in Deep River. Her father was one of ten children, seven of whom are still alive. The clan will be coming in from Connecticut, Florida and California, Vermont and Arizona, as raucous and loving a bunch as there may be anywhere. Old and young will gather to eat hot dogs and hamburgers, compete in volleyball and croquet, and perhaps play cards late into the night as tiki torches blaze in the darkness. There will be laughter, dancing, and music, and maybe some tears, too, for when a family comes together there are memories and regrets and a few sorrows amidst all the joy.

I remember the family reunions of my mother's clan, German immigrants who came to Iowa during the great wave of settlement in the mid-1800s. Leberecht and Alma Kretschmar left their home in Germany for a place where they had heard there was rich, black earth and the promise of a prosperous life. The first winter in their new home they christened that earth with the body of their first child. Long after they, too, were buried in that earth, each October their brood of descendants would gather in the little community center at New Era, in Muscatine County, Iowa. And around fried chicken and green tomato pie and strong coffee they would laugh and marvel at the power of family. The grandchildren would play hide-and-seek under the tall oak trees, and sometimes slide in the cow manure hidden beneath the leaves. The men would play horseshoes and smoke cigars. Aunt Frieda would spit on her linen handkerchief and wipe the dirt off my cheek, and Cousin Margaret would helplessly try to call a family meeting to order. On Saturday, this great grandson of German immigrants will gather with the descendants of Swedes and Brits into which I have married, and I will feel the handkerchief on my cheek and watch for the sparrows making a family, too.

Family Reunion

We are tied
to the ones whose faces
we can no longer remember,
who left their homes for a dream,
and to the ones who watched them go.
And we are tied
to the ones unconceived, unborn,
who have not yet walked joyful
into a May morning,
or heard a sparrow sing wild and free.
And we are tied
to the ones we know too well,
who have fought with us
and said our name with pride,
who have held us in our darkest days
and remembered wrong some ancient folly.
But blood and tears make love
and we are better for this:
the learning to live together,
time's kindness, and the shared dreams,
the gift of laughter, and the wrestled love,
the spilled blood and the tears,

> the spit on the cheek and the arms around,
> and the saving wonder,
> that we are all
> family.

May

Memorial Day

One cold January day, young Frans Petterson swerved to avoid a group of children walking in the road. He drove into a tree, destroying his brand new Nash sedan. He was thrown out of the car and suffered minor injuries, but none of those children were injured. Presumably they grew up to lead productive lives in this little town, as did Frans. He and his wife Elsie lived in a white house set back from Village Street with a huge holly bush by the front steps. He would serve as Town Treasurer and sing in the Congregational Church choir, and Elsie would dote over their one and only son Leonard, her pride and joy. They would watch as Leonard graduated from the University of Maine and then fall in love and eventually marry his bride Catherine on a beautiful June day. Then he was off to war, serving with the Marines in the Pacific. Months later, on his way to Okinawa he was promoted to First Lieutenant. But on June 6, 1945, during the invasion of that little island, he was killed by a sniper's bullet, just days shy of his wedding anniversary.

    The Purple Heart awarded to him could not completely console his grieving parents. After Frans died, I would occasionally visit Elsie and see Leonard's framed picture on the bureau. Elsie carried a sadness through her life and seemed burdened by loneliness and fearful about the unpredictability of an otherwise lovely world. Always she would invite me to come and cut branches of holly to decorate the church at Christmas, and I couldn't help but think of the poignant words of the old English carol, "The holly bears a prickle as sharp as any thorn; And Mary bore sweet Jesus Christ on Christmas Day in the morn."

    I think of Leonard Petterson every Memorial Day, when the citizens of our town gather for a parade down Main Street, ending at the town green. Again this Monday they were there: the fife and drum corps, the scouts, the fire department, a host of veterans wearing remnants of their old uniforms. I waved at my granddaughter with her green saxophone in the elementary school band just behind the oldest of the old soldiers seated on a bench. I watched them salute as a squad of sailors fired a volley in memory of Deep River's sons who had died in battle. A white rose was laid near our "Liberty monument" for each of those remembered dead, including Leonard Petterson. Later I would hug my granddaughter, tell her how wonderful the band sounded, and then she would head home to her house on Village Street, the one where once a great holly bush stood guard by the front door, with prickles sharp as any thorn.

Memorial Day

We stand
in a morning full of bird songs
and a wind ruffling the treetops
as a bugle cries
as if night, not morning, had come.
And so we must cry, all of us,
for those whose day has ended:
the old mother,
her son's picture pressed against her chest,
the child whose father's voice fades to a whisper,
the boyhood friend who wonders
why it was not he who walked
that valley of the shadow of death.
Today the names are called,
and a few still remember
the jaunty turn of the head,
the stolen kiss in the woods behind the cemetery,
the summer night of naked joy by the river
as fireflies rose into the sky
like a dream.
So we keep them in our hearts,
those dreams our world has lost
in heroes' gallantry—

flesh of our flesh,
bright minds and tender lovers,
with us now only in the wind
ruffling the tall trees
this sweet morning.

June

*J*une

Jack-in-the-Pulpit

June has come, with its long afternoons and the deepest green of the year. The warm, settled, summer days have yet to come, and the roses, usually in full bloom by now, are just beginning to break out of their tight buds. And the hillside laurel, which by now normally decks the landscape as if a wedding were about to take place, is late this year, too. But the iris and rhododendron are glorious, and here and there other surprises have begun to reveal themselves.

Hidden at the edge of the terrace are lovely pink stalks of wood hyacinth, and the trillium has opened its secret blooms deep in the shade where no one would ever see it if they didn't know where to look. Today or tomorrow I will take a walk in Canfield Woods to see if I have missed the lady slippers where they come and go so quickly in a wet, shady grove just off a turn in the trail. It is a challenge to catch these seasonal visitors at the moment they appear. Wait too long and they are gone. That is what happened, I think, to the jack-in-the-pulpit that grows near our back door. Away for a long weekend, we returned to find little Jack limp and shriveled under his three-leaf cover.

I have always especially loved jack-in-the-pulpits. I have vague memories of my grandmother, but one of the clearest is walking down the path behind her little house to look for the jack-in-the-pulpits in the shade. She would lift the curving green leaf and smile as she pointed to little "Jack" peeking out from his shelter, almost as if we had found a friend who had once disappeared and now come back. And we had.

Jack-in-the-Pulpit

Some treasures
are shy visitors,
hiding in shadows
or peering at us
from their secret dwellings.
Busy at our important labors,
we lumber past
these gentle faces
that will not be with us long
and miss
their tender blessing.

June

Heart Berries

Thursday is June's full moon—the Strawberry Moon. The name comes from our Native Americans, who knew that the season for gathering these sweet, red berries was a brief and wonderful time, and perhaps they celebrated by feasting under the month's wondrous full moon. Some of them called these fruits "heart-berries," and it's not difficult to figure out why if you hold one in your hand and look at it. They cherished these little fruits as one of the earth's first and sweetest gifts. Even modern scientists agree that strawberries are good for the heart, help reduce blood pressure, and may even have anti-aging properties.

Last Sunday afternoon our local historical society had its annual Strawberry Social in the carriage house across the street. They served strawberry shortcake the correct way, with biscuits and not sponge cake, and it was topped with real cream whipped by the president of the society who has been the official whipper for many years. For many years one of the old members actually grew the strawberries in the field back behind the old Stone House. Everyone always hoped that the berries would ripen in time for the festival, and that the day for picking would be fair and gentle. Now, I think, they get the fruit from the local grocery store, and that is a little disappointing, even though I ate the whole shortcake and licked the plate.

These days you can get strawberries almost year-round, as you can peaches, asparagus, blueberries and tomatoes. It is a luxury we take for granted, even though these gifts of earth don't quite taste the same when they are shipped thousands of miles and are bred for travel-hardiness instead of flavor. No winter strawberry tastes like ones you can pick yourself. When my children were little, we would wait for some sunny June day and head off to the strawberry field to pick a box full. Later those berries would become jams and pies and topping for shortcake; and some would be frozen for a cold, gray day when we needed a taste of summer. But the best ones were those eaten right there in the field, warm, sweet— the ones which left a red ring around your mouth—the ones which made your heart glad to be alive.

Heart Berries

We weary of the bitterness,
the aching disappointment
when a hopeful day
turns tasteless on our lips.
Then some green morning
a red heart shows among the leaves,
warm as the sun.
And this glory that fills
our mouth,
is light itself,
and joy,
and June explodes
for one bright moment,
runs down our cheek,
drips on chin and fingers,
makes us red with desire.
Then we are child,
the world ripe before us,
and, for a moment,
we grow sweet
again.

June

Pomp and Circumstance

For the first time in over sixty years, a graduation took place on the stage of the old Town Hall Auditorium. The last crop of high school graduates who scrawled their signatures on the backstage wall are mostly gone, and these 54 sixth graders still have a while to go before they march in to Pomp and Circumstance to get their high school diplomas. But last night's was a signal moment nonetheless. Under the grand chandelier in the domed ceiling above them, wistful parents and grandparents leaned forward in their seats to watch their bright-eyed, suddenly grown-up looking young men and women march across the stage to receive their "certificates of promotion" to Middle School.

One of them was my perfect granddaughter. There will be other rites of passage throughout her life, as there have been for most of us. She will fixate over her outfit and peer out at a gathered audience to catch the eye of someone who loves her. I know that most of the time, that person she looks for will be someone other than me. Still, I will be there to add my applause and cheers, and sometimes my prayers, as she steps out to graduate, or perform in a concert or play, or get married, or deliver a doctoral thesis, or have a baby. And I hope I will be there, too, at some of those passages that happen quietly, unnoticed by the rest of the world.

These occasions allow us stop and remember how quickly it goes, for all of us. We recall our own passages: the day my voice cracked for the first time in Bill Burton's basement; an unexpected kiss from sweet Norma on a science field trip; riding down a country road in my first, oil-burning, car; watching my grandmother slowly die. And then I remember this: Once, in 7th grade, we were asked to write something about an animal. Most of the kids wrote about cats and dogs. I wrote a poem about lemmings. The teacher gave me a zero, because she didn't think it was possible that a 7th grader could come up with something that original. I felt the sudden turning of the world, the one into the heart of darkness. People hurt us, disbelieve in us. We feel betrayed. Pomp and Circumstance helps me come out of it again.

Pomp and Circumstance

Who is there watching
as I make such a crossing?
Not just the walk across the stage,
the hand stretched out to mine
in salute, or pride, or sympathy.
But the steps I take
into what I cannot know.
Who is there
who knows the price I have paid
for this,
who has seen me through
the tender losses
and dares to tell me that there is
some goodness yet to come?
And if I make some passage today,
if I leave a part of myself behind
as I seek a new place to be,
will you give me a day of roses to remember,
a rustling in honeysuckle so sweet
that the world will stop and smile,
a kiss on my cheek, salted with tears?

And when I make the last of my crossings,
    who will be there watching?
    Will you call out my name,
so that some joy will linger in the air?

June

June Night

The carnival set up on the ball field down the street last weekend. We walked over on Friday evening, one of the sweet, long days of the year. We watched our granddaughters race from ride to ride, giggling as they whipped around on the Tilt-a-Whirl and Cobra. The youngest persuaded her dad to go with her on the Ferris Wheel and something called the Sizzler, and it was a good thing that she didn't ask me. Things that make me dizzy and sick to my stomach have lost most of their appeal for me.

I used to like these things better than I do now—especially the joy of being with friends and sharing an adrenalin rush as we went spinning around, rising and falling. But I've had some misadventures on these things, too. A few years ago when my own kids were young, I was standing at the gate to one of the rides—a kind of gigantic pendulum—waiting for the screaming to cease. As the kids came racing off the ride, one of them erupted his yet undigested hot dog and cotton candy all over my shoes. And then there was the time when my wife and I were at one of the huge theme parks in Florida, and we wound up on something called "the Tower of Terror." It was an elevator ride to the top of a several-story structure, and when you got to the top, the whole thing made a precipitous drop. At the end of the ride, I raced around to get in line to do it again, missing the fact that my wife was crying and shaking on a bench down below. That took something of the thrill away.

And thrills are the attraction of a carnival, no doubt. But for me, now, the things that thrill me most have changed. This weekend we went to the carnival to eat cheeseburgers and fried dough, as well as to watch our granddaughters in their joy. Lily won a life-size inflatable green alien for ringing the bell on that sledge-hammer midway game, and there was a sweet nostalgia about being there in the long light of a June evening as young teenagers held hands and imagined being in love. Phyllis and I walked home, hand in hand, hoping we might catch a glimpse of the rose-breasted grosbeak on the feeder by the back door.

June Night

The carnival has come to town,
and we are pulled in by its magic:
music, and the cries of midway barkers,
laughter under the glittering lights,
and wild, unfettered screams of joy
rising in a moment of sheer abandon,
and once again the world is young.
But she and I turn toward home
as rose streaks the sky
and the first stars welcome the night.
We look for fireflies on the meadow,
listen for the tender song of crickets,
the soft ringing of wind chimes,
and perhaps the flutter of wings
as a bird seeks a roost in the trees.
We pause here, at the last edge of day
at the fulcrum of the year
and are content
with our simple thrills
as the earth spins us round again
together.

July

July

Fireworks

The Fourth of July is an American holiday, a pause in the midst of summer to celebrate the founding of this nation. Roadside stands not only offer piles of watermelons and not quite native tomatoes to provide for family picnics, but also boxes of sparklers, bottle rockets, cherry bombs, fountains and firecrackers that are designed to make maximum amounts of noise and smoke and a few glorious explosions of light at nightfall. As a child, my mother warned us against such things ("you could blow a finger off with one of those!") though at least once my father brought back a stash to our home in Iowa from a place across the border in Missouri where they were legal. You could see the bright explosions reflected in his joyous eyes.

If we really wanted fireworks, we'd head out to a field on the edge of town and, with hundreds of other families, spread out our blankets and have a picnic. As the sun settled on the western horizon we became restless for darkness. Fireflies twinkled over us as the stars began to come out, one by one, and at last it was night. We stretched out on our backs and watched spectacular displays erupt over us—great fiery chrysanthemums and waterfalls of light, booming gloriously as ashes drifted down and settled on us. Never was a child so happy as when the grand finale burst and shuddered in the sky.

In these older years, I confess, I eschew the traffic and the hungry mosquitoes and usually avoid whatever local fireworks displays may tempt me. My Fourth of July is marked by other celebrations. I walk in the back yard and check the sour cherry tree, hoping that the blue jays will have left enough for a Fourth of July pie. I gather the sugar snap peas in the loose tail of my shirt and sit in the shade to see if the oriole will come down to feast on the mulberry tree which we let grow by accident. Across the street the bright orange day lilies line the street, on schedule again for their Fourth of July visitation. They toss their heads in the breeze, like fireworks.

Fireworks

High in the deep sky
great showers of light explode,
fountains and blossoms
filling the darkness.
Their boom and thunder shake the ground,
stirring a wide-eyed child to laugh with wonder.
But somewhere another child cowers,
face buried in a terrified mother's arms
as she waits for silence to cover her.
There is no delight for her,
no joy of picnic and celebration
in the ancient percussion of death
dropping from the sky.
We wish her freedom from this.
We would give her a bright summer day
of games in grassy fields
and sweet starry nights of gentle dreams—
a world where the only explosions
would be the flash and fire
of orange blossoms waving
in the peaceful morning
of a new day.

July

A Baseball Dream

There we were, looking down on that wonderful emerald green field in the midst of the concrete city. It was Fenway Park in Boston, a mystical place where a summer night means baseball. We were up above third base, in seats which were a gift from my sons who had heard that the Chicago Cubs would be coming to New England for a rare inter-league game between these two ill-fated teams. I grew up rooting for the Cubs, as had my father, believing that someday they might have a winning team. It has not happened yet. In fact, it has been 106 years since the Cubs won the World Series. But on this night in July the Cubs' pitcher was throwing a no-hitter into the eighth inning. We, these men tied together by blood and story, joined in the chants and cheers and watched night fall over the great green wall in left field where so much Boston magic has taken place.

I thought of my father-in-law, who grew up cheering for these Red Sox, and especially for his idol, the great Ted Williams. In some sense, my father-in-law was a boy who never grew up. He dreamed of playing baseball forever, and once he had a chance. He was signed by the Brooklyn Dodgers, and he made his way up through the minor leagues for a while. He was a star for the Sheboygan Indians and remembers playing for the Greenwood (Mississippi) Dodgers, where in the heat of the Gulf summer they played in short pants as the girls in the grandstand hooted. Once, in spring training, he caught a fly ball that Willie Mays hit to the wall in center field. But because of an injury, he never made it to the Big Leagues. Still, he got farther than most of us who dream of such things. My father-in-law died last night, still reliving those memories and those dreams.

A. Bartlett Giamatti, former president of Yale University who was later the Commissioner of Baseball, once said that baseball "tells us that as much as you travel and far as you go, out to the green frontier, the purpose is to get back home, back to where the others are." My wife's dad has been leading off third base most of his life. Maybe at last he's sliding into home. On that night last week in Boston, when the Cubs won 2-0, there was almost a no-hitter. But the real glory of the game was up in the stands, on the third base side, where a father and his sons were together, ball caps on our heads, screaming our lungs out, remembering where home was.

A Baseball Dream

We played catch in the back yard,
my father, tongue clenched in his teeth,
left-handed mitt on his hand,
and I, a would-be second baseman,
who lived through his stories.
Once he met an over-the-hill Babe Ruth—
the great Bambino—
barnstorming through town
for a few bucks and, mostly,
for the love of it.
Some lucky Iowa boy
could be on his team
for one night, they said,
by heaving a baseball
over the tallest building in town.
My Dad leaned back and threw it—
heart and soul he threw it—
up, up, higher than he ever dared dream.
He recalls that the ball nearly went over,
bounced against the highest ledge,
and fell back to earth.
I am still waiting to catch it.

July

Summer Rain

"Rain, rain, go away, come again some other day!" Children have been singing that old chant for hundreds of years, especially on summer days when they wanted to be outside playing. Most of us still wish for sunny days, and these are often the setting for the happiest days of our lives. But rain, too, is good and necessary. The peppers in our garden have been drooping and even the morning glories climbing the fence have been limp as they wait for rain after a long stretch of dry weather. By this time in July, too, the grass in a hundred lawns is looking brown and thirsty. So it is as if the world was uttering a long, sweet, "Aaaah!" when yesterday it rained at last.

In the book The Outermost House, Henry Beston's classic description of a year spent in a spare cabin amid the sand dunes of Cape Cod, he notes that there are "three great elemental sounds in nature": the sound of rain, the sound of wind in the trees, and the sound of the ocean on the beach. There is something wondrous about the sound of approaching rain: the whisper in the treetops on a nearby hill, the swish of car tires passing on the street, the blip of drops hitting the water of the creek or the pond around the corner. Last night we slept to the patter of rain against the window glass, a rhythmic, sweet sound that reminds us of a primal truth: that rain is life. We, earth creatures, are mostly water. And we live on the only planet yet discovered in a vast and lonely universe that is wet.

Sometimes the wetness is annoying. As a matter of fact, I was a block away from home walking our dogs when the rains began. It came as sheets of heavy, soaking rain, and by the time we got home, we were wet and soaked, too. The dogs had a good shake in the kitchen, and I changed into dry clothes. But this morning, in shorts and bare feet, I resisted the temptation to run for cover. I felt the wet grass between my toes, savored the cool leaves brushing against my legs and splattering my shirt and pants, laughed at the rivulets running down my face. I was alive with summer rain.

Summer Rain

I am wet with life,
slippery as morning.
I walk through a green world
where the most precious of gifts
falls from the sky.
The earth drinks deeply
of such goodness
as something like a song
ripples through the tall trees.
We wish the summer rain away,
seek shelter, wait for sun,
when we could walk uncovered,
dripping with joy
and drenched with glory.
O sweet rain,
moisten the dry earth.
Soften my thirsty heart.
Be gentle! Be life!

July

Comes the Parade

Last weekend was Deep River's annual "Ancient Muster," the largest one-day gathering of fife and drum corps in the world. It's been happening annually in this little town on a July Saturday since 1953, and sporadically before that since 1879. The boom and rattle of drums and the high-pitched music of fifes fills the air all weekend as travelling bands from as far away as Switzerland gather in friendly competition and an all-night jam session, called a "tattoo," on the local ball field. Listening to fife and drum music for a whole weekend is a bit much for some, but most of us at least drag our lawn chairs down to Main Street for the Saturday parade.

A parade stirs childlike excitement in the stodgiest of souls. And our parade has the usual side attractions. There are balloon vendors and hot dog peddlers, and you can buy T-shirts and hats and badges to prove that you've been to beautiful downtown Deep River. A portable barbecue smoker set up business in the parking lot behind the hardware store, and a host of curious children were gleefully grossed out to see the decapitated hog's head mounted on the sign over the stand. But then the moment came for which everyone waited: the flashing lights of the police escort, the snapping flags in the morning breeze, and the local drum corps stepping into view with a rousing version of the Battle Hymn of the Republic.

There are marchers dressed as sailors and pirates, some in bright formal uniforms with brass buttons and tricorn hats. Kids on bicycles ride in and out of the spaces between the bands, smiling at the joy of being in the parade, too. Muskets fire into the sky; we jump in our seats, laughing with the surprise of it. Perhaps we're laughing with a joy that we can still be surprised—still giggle like children as the parade passes by. In the musical Hello, Dolly, the main character, Dolly Levi, a widow, realizes that it's time to move on with a life where there's been too much sadness and solitude. "Before the parade passes by," she sings, "I've gotta get some life back into my life." "I wanna feel my heart coming alive again," she belts out with gusto. On Saturday, we got a little taste of the parade that's waiting for all of us.

Comes the Parade

We were young once
and the band was far down the street
around a corner, invisible,
and we waited
watched
listened
for the distant thunder,
the flutter of trumpets
a hopeful, throaty cheer from those
who could already see it.
At last they came,
shaking the earth,
gleaming with reflected light
and carrying the world along
to the beat of an endless march,
then stepped along, away,
a passing dream,
the memory of a shining splendor
that once we saw.
We are older now,
still peering into the distance
standing on tiptoe and looking for the band
to come again and raise a pulse in us.

But I hope for this:
that we may step out into a breathless morning
and see a child down the street
glimpse something shining in us
bright as a sweet trumpet's song,
maybe even hear the tap of drums
which is the march beat of our life,
and believe that we are the parade.

July

First Tomato

I have been watching this momentous change for several days. One or two of the swollen green tomatoes hanging near the garden fence looked like they were starting to blush a bit. I waited. Early this cool morning as I filled the bird feeders, I looked up to see an unmistakable bright red globe peeking out from the heavy green foliage. The first glorious tomato of the year! If there is a reason to grow a garden, this must be it.

Of course I plant other things, too. I plant lettuce and peas as early as I can, just to be able to enjoy the first Spring produce after a long, cold winter. Then comes the procession of green beans and summer squash, Swiss chard and cucumbers. I just now see purple eggplants the size of golf balls promising something bigger and better in a few weeks. But a ripe tomato is the prize worth all the stiff muscles and sweat it takes to wish them into being from the time those little dry seeds are planted in March and the little seedlings are set under the basement lights.

A tomato is more than a tomato, of course. Most of us get our share of tomatoes in salsa and spaghetti sauce and enjoy them immensely. My grandmother and mother both spent long hot summer afternoons peeling and chopping tomatoes and peppers and stirring them into immense pots of chili sauce, which were ladled into glass jars and boiled some more before being set aside in long rows on our cellar shelves in preparation for our winter tables. Out in the black soil of our Iowa garden, my father grew Beefsteaks and Big Boys and Rutgers Improved, long and sprawling, and one July afternoon he would wave me out to join him in the chest-high vines. He would bend down and twist a huge red fruit off and hand it to me, then pick one for himself. Together we would bite into those first tomatoes, and the warm juice would run down our chins and soak into our shirts as we shared a most simple and wonderful joy. Heaven will be like that, I think: a summer day, a mouthful of tomato, my father's smile.

First Tomato

There are crickets chirping
In the long afternoon,
and the first katydids rehearsing
their summer song.
It is the incidental music,
the score of these tender days,
when a tomato waits
for an old memory to ripen.
It is there in the odor of earth,
in the bright, musky scent of tomato leaves,
when the fading sepia image of a tall man,
sunburned, strong, T-shirted,
reaches through the years
for one red fruit.
He bites into it, grins, looks up at me
these decades later
and hundreds of miles away
from that sunny Iowa field
where once I learned joy.
"There," he says,
somewhere close,
"It's for you."

August

August

Mountaintop

I carried a walking stick with me this weekend. It was a sturdy thing, hand-decorated by an Adirondack Mountain wood-carver many years ago. Jim had used it year after year, and Friday the group of friends who had hiked with him over the years were heading up to New Hampshire once again to laugh and eat and enjoy the mountain air together. Jim was 78 years old when he had the idea of inviting a group to join him on the trails of the White Mountains; and that year we loaded packs and clambered up to the rustic Zealand Falls Hut, situated on the edge of a waterfall. It was cold and rainy, and we got wet, sore, and tired. One of us almost fell off a ledge, and the streams were so swollen that a few members of the group had to strip down and wade through the water carrying a bundle of their clothes over their heads. It was wonderful.

 We've been doing these annual hikes for 25 years now; and Jim kept coming, too, until he died a couple of years ago at age 99. Lately we've taken to staying at slightly cushier lodgings (we like indoor plumbing and electricity to charge our phones, even if there is no cellular service deep in the mountains). And some of us, who are as gray on top as the mountain summits, choose kinder and shorter trails for our adventures. But we are still drawn to these magnificent places by the bond of friendship and a deep and primal desire to immerse ourselves for a while in the awesomeness of nature.

We humans are drawn to mountains and seashores, to the brims of lakes and rivers, for our souls' sakes. There we can stand at the edge of something vast and mysterious and look into endless distances. We feel the surge and retreat of the deep waters that resonate with the very tides of our bodies. We stand on mountain ridges and look down upon circling hawks and the minuteness of highways that dwindle like bloodless human arteries into the insignificance of our noisy and distracted lives. In these places we find, if but for a moment, a peace. Last weekend Jim's walking stick made it to the summit of Mt. Moosilauke. I hope that Jim made it there, too.

Mountaintop

We stand in silence,
as close as we can get
to the edge of a great immensity.
We look out at endless ridges of stone,
or to the hidden thing just beyond the horizon.
We wait, unmoving,
held by wonder,
not so much humbled by our own small size
as enlarged by the girth and glory
of what is all around us.
We stay there
waiting to remember
what we have forgotten
in the rush of our exhausting days:
that we live among mountains
and listen to the pulse of oceans
in our bones and blood,
that we come to ancient rivers that beckon us
to greater waters than we have ever known.
We find some narrow trail
to take us to these sacred places,

find others who would go with us
to that reverence and quiet
where life is offered,
like a gift.

August

Shooting Stars

The days are still full of summer, but the nights are telling us that things are changing. The dusk settles upon us earlier now, and with it the loud songs of the cicadas and crickets and katydids, almost a din resounding from their hiding places in the woods around us. To the insects themselves, this may be a love song. But the lyrics I hear are these: "Summer is ending. Summer is ending."

This week has also been a time of celestial omens. A bright perigee full moon, popularly known as a "Super Moon" because of its size, has spilled its silver light over the August landscape just as the greatest meteor shower of the year—the Perseids—has arrived. This happens annually in mid-August, as our small planet sweeps through the remnant of a comet's tail. Some of that tail—particles of ice, rock, and space dust—burn up as they pass through earth's atmosphere. We see them as "shooting stars" in the night. Some scientists speculate that as we watch the streaks of fire across the sky, we might actually be seeing a replay of how water arrived on earth during the millennia of this strange blue planet's formation.

Cosmic origins aside, these annual meteor showers signal that the arc of another year has turned toward autumn. Monday we went out in the back yard and tipped back in our Adirondack chairs to watch the show and to cherish for another moment the sweetness of a summer night. With that moon shining, there weren't many meteors to see. But one glorious streak of light did autograph our night, reminding me of another summer. My sons were little boys then, and one August night on vacation we drove through a countryside devoid of street lights or shopping centers. Along a quiet dirt road we pulled over and clambered onto a grassy embankment with a couple of blankets and stretched out on our backs to watch what most of the world was missing. We said nothing to each other except for an occasional gasp or shout or giggle as the miracle unfolded. Stars were in our eyes.

Shooting Stars

Nothing is fixed.
Everything changes.
The ancient stars
stretched across the heavens
have kept an order through the eons.
I was born to see what ancients saw:
a wondrous permanence,
the Great Dipper pointing to Polaris—
a guide to ships and sleepless wayfarers.
We have sought the stars for this,
like old Orion, hunting endlessly
for something that would stay.
And then on this moonlit August night,
even the steadfast stars seem to burn and fly,
like summer, like time,
like all we hold precious.
They flash before us for a moment,
leaving a gleaming trail across the darkness,
then are gone.
But there remains a memory to haunt us,
a signature of lingering light—
or perhaps a bright dream

of lying on a meadow's edge not so long ago
as crickets chirped a love song
and little children, watching stars rain fire,
made a silver wish.

August

Summer Afternoon

Now in the midst of August we are glad for simple, ordinary hours. There are a few left this summer, days to savor sunlight and silence and a little time to sit and watch clouds drift by. Henry James, a 19th century American philosopher, once observed that the two most beautiful words in the English language may be these: "summer afternoon." Those words should be spoken softly, almost dreamily, as if we were Mole and Rat in The Wind in the Willows, drifting down the river in their little boat, glad to be alive even for just a little while.

Of course it is possible to be content in the dead of winter, too. But here, in Connecticut in these waning days of August, we dwell in a season of life that asks little of us. No shoveling the walks, no heavy clothes to put on and take off, no stoking of the fire. It is not necessary to hurry from the house to the car. It is enough to mosey along, and sometimes just to stand there, bare feet in the grass, grateful for loveliness all around. And this loveliness today is bright with color.

Winter is painted with a palate of gray and brown and white. By February we are hungry for a world that is green, and the purples and reds displayed in the promises of the garden catalogs seem slightly lurid, almost erotic. But here, in the heart of August, the zinnias and sunflowers are all joy. Enormous scarlet and magenta dahlias and pink hibiscus line the garden fence. And marigolds, bright as school buses, wave in the breeze. What a gift to be surrounded by such color! Dogs and cats and many other mammals, it is said, are somewhat color blind. How sad for them! Birds and butterflies see the colors we do, but ultraviolet light, too. Watch a hummingbird flit from the scarlet runner beans to the purple butterfly bush, and you'll be a believer. Listen carefully, and you may hear them whir by, singing "Summer afternoon, Summer afternoon!"

Summer Afternoon

Dream a summer afternoon
and save it
for some winter night
whose barren threads are loveless,
cold, and gray as death.
This dream will fill the thinnest air
with a perfume of marigold,
pungent as the warm earth,
and it will calm the whistling wind
with the drone of an August night,
the mysterious orchestra of insects
playing their sweet concerto while they can,
a love song under stars.
And there will be colors,
so gaudy and wild that we will laugh
and gather blazing bouquets
glorious as any hearthfire
to paint the walls of our sleeping.
And the bees will follow us,
drunk with pink and red and gold,
carrying their secrets to a place
where they will work their holy alchemy.
And this golden honey, given and kept,

will be for us a taste
of warm and lazy afternoons,
a luminous rainbow of a dream to feed us
until our summer comes again.

August

Fair

The last weekend of summer, just before the school buses start running, is always the Chester Fair. The Fair Season in Connecticut runs from late August into October. It is a lingering remnant of the agrarian communities that once flourished up and down our river valleys, where time was measured by planting and sowing, cultivating and harvest. As the growing season came to an end, folks would gather to celebrate with food and music, displays of their produce and good-natured competition to prove who was the best in the land.

Now many of these fairs have become seasonal carnivals, with an emphasis on rides and midway games. But our Chester Fair still has barns where a dwindling number of farmers bring their cattle and goats, where teams of enormous horses go against each other at pulling great sleds loaded with concrete blocks, where proud gardeners show off their finest vegetables and flowers, and where judges sample double-crust apple pies, chocolate cakes, jellies, jams, and pickles to give someone bragging rights in our small little corner of the world. Yet this is serious business. Years ago I knew a man who assured himself of winning a blue ribbon at the Fair by entering something that nobody else would think of entering, at least here in Connecticut: he grew okra.

Make no mistake: I come to eat fried dough sprinkled with cinnamon and sugar, maybe have a roasted ear of corn or a roll overflowing with sausage and peppers. But always we find our way to the barns on the edge of the fairgrounds where farm kids are shearing their sheep and town kids are begging their parents to let them pick out a rabbit to take home as a pet. This year we also headed over to the juvenile display area, where kids enter their favorite hobby collections and artwork. There we found a prize-winning painting done by our extremely talented 12-year-old granddaughter, who also won a ribbon for her photograph of a marigold and a blue ribbon for her San Marzano plum tomatoes. Bring on the fried dough!

Fair

The massive horses stand in shade,
snorting and tossing their heads
as they wait to be led up the dusty ring,
to heave together against a weary weight
as straw-hatted men sit in the bleachers
and shake their heads with respect.
A child steps to pat the nose
of one slick-maned, beauteous beast,
and the great thing pulls away,
as if it knows that this is not a day
for gentle gestures.
Today prizes will be lavished
on strutting roosters and pampered sheep,
on perfect tomatoes and prodigious dahlias,
on pies that look too good to eat,
and on some stomping, sweating team
of Percherons or Belgians.
But I would like just one old barn someplace
where the smell of roasting corn can drift and fill the air,
where a child could win a big blue ribbon
for kindness, or for joy,
where a funny-looking goat could earn a prize
just for being loved the most.

September

September

Carry Me Home, Old River

The trip is short, not more than a half an hour or so, down this beautiful river to the place of wonders. We were invited again this year to travel by boat with friends to witness the great murmuration of swallows. Each year, beginning at the end of August, a majestic flock of tree swallows makes its way south on its annual migration. And here, in the long reeds of an estuary island near the mouth of the Connecticut River, they come to make a nightly roost. As we ride the tidal current, we wait for the hour of sunset, when perhaps half a million birds gather from miles around. We watch them, circling overhead in dancing waves of life, moving as if they were one great winged creature, guided by some invisible force. Then they drop silently, suddenly, and it is over. The sun applauds, painting the water vermillion and rose, as we turn for home.

    Out on the river, there is a kind of silence in spite of the boat's motor. The wind is loud, and conversation is difficult. And the deep water beating at the sides of the boat collapses into a mighty rush of foam in our wake. But the silence is of the world away from us, the quiet of gulls overhead, and muted laughter from a passing schooner. It is as if the world holds its breath again as the color drains away into an exuberance of stars.

And here we are caught again in the great cycles of time and life. This is the season of the annual migration of swallows, whose ancestors made this trip over the ages, answering a call as powerful to them as it is mysterious to us. But we live amid a host of such mighty forces, too: that little ache in the heart as summer moves into autumn once again; the ebb and flow of the ocean's tide against a waxing moon; the great motion of constellations as Orion rises in the September sky; the migration of children back to school; and the unremitting procession of death and birth, change and decay that mark all joy, all sadness. This is our river, and tonight we feel the ancient call to return again to a place where, for a while, we can roost.

Carry Me Home, Old River

Carry me home, old River,
to the place I have never been,
that place to which I always return.
Sing to me a ballad I can remember,
a song of stars and wind and tide,
a serenade as true as moonlight
when the moon is nowehere to be seen.
Often I have sung my own song,
taken my own singular path
against the traffic of the world.
But in the evening
I feel the pull of blood and tide,
wish to join the tender migration
that binds the starfish and the stars.
So I come to you, boatless,
wishing to bend to your water,
to dip my hands, shoulders, body into your life,
to ride your silver stream
and feel its whisper and thrum,
tuning my own heartbeat to its rhythm.
I seek the place beyond seeing,
the island where the swallows rest,
the place both salt and fresh

at the meeting of all waters,
the ancient home where life begins and ends
in peace.
Carry me there, old River.

September

Girl on the Bus

Boxes of unsharpened pencils and stacks of notebooks fill the store shelves, and kids lugging oversized backpacks line up at the corners waiting for the buses to haul them off to school. These big yellow buses mean September is here, and a new season. And they carry the most precious of cargo. They make us stop and remember. Driving down a long straightaway a couple of days ago, I got caught behind an afternoon bus unloading kids every hundred yards or so. That short stretch of road took an exorbitantly long time to traverse, and I am certain some of the other drivers in the lineup of cars behind me were not quite as patient about the length of their trip.

    My granddaughter reported that she, too, is riding the bus this year. Her new school is a little too far away for her to walk, as she did last year when she attended the elementary school just a few blocks from her house. She developed an aversion to riding the bus several years ago. As a little girl at school for the first time, she got on the bus at the end of the day and was one of the last to get off at the end of a fairly long, circuitous route. The day at school had taken its toll: she fell asleep, slumped down on the seat. The driver could not see her. And it wasn't until the bus pulled into the lot for the night that the driver discovered one tired, scared little girl still on board.

Hopefully, her bus trips will be more pleasant now. I still remember those rides to school in my own youth: Pete the bus driver and his funny welcome, the vague smell of sour milk and old thermoses, the thump of metal lunch boxes and the squeak of wet rubber boots tromping down the aisle in search of a seat. And I hold on to an old shame. One little girl on our bus route lived in a poor house in the woods, and she got on the bus each day with the same clothes and a worn jacket. Her hair was usually tangled, and she always stared at the floor as she made her way toward a seat at the back of the bus. She was usually greeted with smirks, muffled giggles, and rude gestures, such as kids holding their nose as if something smelled bad. Something did, but it wasn't her. It was that nobody, not even I, ever offered her a seat.

Girl on the Bus

Where is she now,
the little one who did not belong
among all the bright, beloved children?
She was an outcast, once,
poor, disheveled, lonely,
who made the long, painful walk every day
to the very back of the bus
waiting for someone to offer her
a place to sit.
If I could find her now,
I hope she would be tall and fair of face,
one whose clear eyes
has forgiven the folly of the world.
I pray that her wounded heart,
scarred by childhood cruelty,
has been healed by a later love,
and welcomed into a kinder world.
If I could find her now,
I would stand as she came by,
invite her to sit by me for a while,
perhaps in a seat by the window
so that she could smile

at the loveliness of the world
and know that on this big bus we share,
there is a place for her,
for everyone.

September

Promise

It is early morning, just before sunrise, and we are walking by the place where the old river road passes over the marsh. The cove is filled with the long, grassy heads of wild rice. No wonder that hundreds of red-winged blackbirds gather here. Along the railroad tracks the chatter of birds is constant, as if a great meeting is in progress. In the open water, swans, geese and ducks awaken, ready to find breakfast in the mud below the surface. They flap their wings excitedly, then turn upside-down to feast, ignorant of the human presence.

Walking along the tracks, the air is rich with the aroma of wild concord grapes. The remnants of acorns decorate the ground under tall oak trees. And here and there long spires of goldenrod reach for the light. September's days slip past this way. Up on the hill the apple trees are heavy with fruit, and down here, by the river, the leaves are already changing. It is cold here in the morning, and we walk quickly toward a new season.

The blackbirds know. Their song is not the joyous trill of April. It is really not a song at all, but the incessant noise of conversation. They chatter, then rise and circle only to descend again into the lush grasses. The prattle of birds goes on. We cannot understand the subject of their communication. Perhaps it is a sound made in assurance that in the failing light and the dying down of things, they are not alone. We seek this too, in some ways. We yearn to find company in the coming of darkness. Some of us hold on to a companion simply out of that fear—that terror of growing old alone. We are creatures who need others, need to hear voices. We take wing, feel the tug and pull of seasons and stars. Sooner or later the time will come when we must go. But we will not do it alone.

Promise

They gather here
in the tall marsh grass
singing a raucous song to the morning.
In blood and bone
they feel autumn's warning,
know the taste of darkness, cold and death.
It will not be long,
this goodness, this grace
of flower and seed.
The grapes are falling,
and the wild asters tell the tale
of a world that forever changes.
Now it is time to gather,
to be a living cloud,
or a congregation uncontained,
murmuring their practiced prayers
before exulting in the gold and green
of September's joyous day.
It seems they hear some secret signal,
then suddenly rise together into the blue
for a precious little while,
as if something should be seen,
or a promise could be made here.

They trust this:
The sun will rise.
The river will run.
We will wing our way together
into some new day.

September

Morning Walk

Now it is dark here at 6 a.m. Though it still feels like night, an internal alarm clock goes off inside me. I stir, then pull myself to my feet, get dressed and head downstairs to begin this new day. I am a keeper of routines. For me, the daily rounds are as comforting as the ancient holy offices of the monastics. I do not call my morning practices elegant names like matins and lauds, but they sustain me in much the same way. I am comforted by the predictable framework that has stitched my life together through years of change. I open the front door, step out to pick up the daily newspaper and wish the world well. Inside again, I turn on the coffee pot, which is a signal to the cats that food is coming. They weave in and out of my path as I jingle the leashes in an attempt to call the dogs for their walk. They come, but reluctantly, in these darker mornings.

Our morning walk may take many different routes. Sometimes the two dogs and I set out across the ball field and the path through the sand pits. It is overgrown now, and my pants get wet going that way. We may follow the railroad tracks along the cove, or go for a run in the old cemetery on top of the hill where a beautiful herald angel atop a tall pillar faces east to watch the sun rise. Often in the dark mornings we stay on the sidewalks in the center of town, where streetlights show the way. That's what we did this morning.

Along this circuit a bus stops in front of the pharmacy in the darkness, and waits a minute as if somebody might show up for a ride. A white pickup turns into the driveway of the doughnut shop. Down the street the lights from inside the corner restaurant reveal a bald man in a leather jacket alone at the counter, bent over a steaming mug of coffee. We turn down a side street, and the noise of the Main St. traffic suddenly falls away. We walk together into the soft whir of crickets and the whisper of a breeze. This morning's quiet is the prize, the gift, of such early rising. It is the silent smile of a day's possibility, the wordless invocation of gratitude, my matins.

Morning Walk

They take me down familiar streets,
suddenly straining at the other end of leashes
for an elusive scent in long grass
or the provocative bark of a distant dog.
I breathe deep, too,
as if there might be something hidden
waiting to be noticed
in these hills and roads of home.
In a comforting window a light goes on,
and I look away as if to avoid intruding
on some intimate awakening.
This quiet time is lovely, healing.
I would not barge into a day without this time,
this tender place—a hollow of expectancy
where something may yet be born,
or an idea rise and circle for a while, like a bird,
or a remembered song of joy stir to life.
So we head into dawn,
looking for something to surprise us:
a tennis ball hiding in the grass,
a heron skimming the treetops,
a runner circling the streets in neon pink shoes,
a crimson leaf flickering by the pond,
like a flame.

October

October

Woolly Bear

It still felt like summer this weekend, but a sure sign of autumn was the Woolly Bear caterpillar (Pyrrharctia isabella) that we found inching its way through the grass. We stopped to take note of this bristly, bi-colored creature, so far removed from us in the network of living things. Yet we hoped it could tell us something about our future. The old lore has it that if the brown band in the middle of the caterpillar is wide, the coming winter will be mild. So we took some comfort, on this sunny September day, to believe that this little moth-to-be was offering good news for the cold months ahead.

 The future is always a great unknown, and perhaps that is why even intelligent creatures like humans still consult groundhogs and caterpillars to give us a glimpse at what may lie ahead. Some of these old tales may have some truth in fact, at least when it comes to weather. I have always been told that a halo around a winter moon means that snow is coming. Yesterday's rosy sunrise cautioned "Red sky in morning, sailors take warning." And today it is raining. But some other prognosticating practices may just be wishful thinking. My Great Aunt Anna hid an almond in the Christmas rice pudding, promising that whomever found it in their bowl would have wealth or love in the new year. And my grandmother had the mysterious power to read the future in coffee grounds left in the bottom of a drained cup. In her visions, the future always held something good.

Of course the future is not always benevolent. Some would say that the universe is remarkably indifferent to our personal well-being. An article in Sunday's New York Times tried to put one person's life in the context of the universe. The writer surmised that after his own death, his remains would begin to be re-absorbed into the earth's mold. Within 67 years of his death, the last person with a living memory of him would also die. Within 10,000 years ecological disaster and disease would wipe out most of the human population of earth, and in seven million years or so an asteroid would collide with our planet and send it spinning on a slow journey into the sun. Just over three billion years from now a tiny speck of what used to be a human person would become a falling star in another galaxy. Perhaps this inevitable doom is too dreary a prospect for a bright Autumn day. Maybe that's why it cheers us up to imagine that a caterpillar can help us dream a soft winter and an early spring.

Woolly Bear

You travel a journey in the world
by inches,
crawling toward winter
with a promise you cannot know.
We will die, both of us, soon enough,
and autumns will come and go
as sure as the geese will fly.
But for this little moment
of sun and splendor,
I would believe your sweet forecast
that winter will be kind and soft,
and that spring will come soon,
and that like you, little Isabella,
I will one day take wing and fly,
or live some hidden dream
beyond my present sight.
We creep together through this green season
bearing an assurance—
or at least a wish—
that though cold days may come,
we shall all be well.

October

Train Tracks

October in New England is defined by its colors—the bright oranges, reds, and yellows that paint the hills and valleys. For me it has always been smells, too. Years ago it was the smell of burning leaves that perfumed every October afternoon. Still, autumn is redolent with earth smells, the sweetness of decay and the ripeness of apples fallen in the long grass. In the autumn wind sometimes you can catch a whiff of the sea, or perhaps the merest hint of winter in the night air. But the sounds of autumn are there, too. I smile at the familiar rustling of leaves on the streets. And I paused this morning to watch an arrow of geese passed over the treetops, honking some kind of message and massaging the air with the beating of wings.

Here in Deep River we hear another sound: the whistle of an old steam locomotive as it makes its way up and down the river valley. For generations the sound of a train whistle has been a haunting sound. It has been a harbinger of change and loss, a yearning for something beyond our sight, or a longing for those who have left us. Autumn, too, has about it this sense of lament. Even in its sweetness, it sings a song of departure, of endings. It is a season of memories about those who have taken some train far away from us, or of opportunities we have missed and of days that will come no more.

But I walk the railroad tracks remembering the boy that I once was, waiting on the platform of the station, waiting for the rumble in the distance, the plume of smoke, the bright light of the approaching engine. It would roar into view, sleek and gleaming, then churn to a stop. These trains had magical names, like the Rocky Mountain Rocket and the Denver Zephyr. I never got to travel on one of them, but I always dreamed that they were bound for glory. And they made me think that in this world where everything was possible, I might be bound for glory, too.

Train Tracks

We would kneel in the gravel
and carefully place our pennies
on the shining steel rails,
then wait in the trees
for a great engine to come thundering by,
flattening our coins into good luck charms.
We would pocket those copper discs
and they would carry us away
to the golden lands of our dreams.
We always wished, then,
to go somewhere else,
imagining that life would carry us away
to a place past prairies and mountains,
a place where we could find something—
perhaps fame, or romance, or glory—
beyond the long bend in the tracks.
Today it is quiet as I walk the twin rails
that curve past water and woods.
Amid a flurry of yellow leaves
I am a boy again,
hearing in the wind a far-away whistle.
Though I am content in this good place,
I reach in my pocket for a penny

and place it on the track.
I leave it there behind me,
offering it to someone
who may walk these rails tomorrow
and need to pick up a dream.

October

Autumn Crown

The huge pile of leaves in our front yard is a product of the great old maple that stands guard over the south side of the house. The bright leaves have been swirling down for a few weeks now, a process accelerated by the weekend's wind and rain. Actually, the pile is so big because my granddaughter and her friend spent a few hours raking it high enough so that they could do satisfactory dives and flips into it. Wild giggling followed, then more raking, then more jumping. Then I took a leap, too.

The great fall of leaves brings the loveliest of seasons to New England. The first glimpse of autumn comes in August, when a flash of red appears in the roadside sumac or the woodbine climbing a stone wall. Up north the change of colors begins in earnest in September, and where we are, near the mouth of the Connecticut River, the peak of foliage color may not come until the end of October. We savor this, even though it is a change that leads to winter. The scientific explanation is that as the days shorten and the light dwindles, the green chlorophyll in the leaves can't continue to feed the tree and eventually the tree stops producing it. As chlorophyll disappears, we begin to see other pigments which hide during the green of the year. Orange and yellow and red make their show at last.

Sometimes we see this in people, too: when darkness gathers and the hard seasons come, our colors may turn the brightest. Often in those difficult times the human spirit shines with its greatest beauty. Many years ago I spent an October afternoon with an old professor at his summer cabin high up on the bank of the Housatonic River. He was a famous historian, a great author, at the twilight of his life. It had turned cold, and the little man stood bundled up in a heavy coat, his small round glasses glinting in the failing sunlight. The autumn wind tousled his mane of snow-white hair as leaves flew around us. "Some people get depressed melancholy when autumn comes and everything dies down," he said looking at the multi-hued hills across the river. Then he grinned as I'll always remember him: "But what a way to go!"

Autumn Crown

I have come now to the autumn,
and I see that my hair
has turned gray with time.
Around me the October world
is making its way toward winter,
and on a thousand hills
there is one more surge of life
before the cold days arrive.
The grandfather trees,
their roots deep in ancient soil,
seem to smile,
knowing that it is fine to stand
in the fading light
wearing an autumn crown.
I have earned my gray, these years,
but sometimes I think
that it would be a lovely thing
to walk some crisp afternoon
with hair of red and gold,
a crown of joy to shine
in the fading light.

October

Morning Glory

The long, balmy days were sure to end eventually. This has been a gentle summer of soft days and cool nights, and this golden autumn has continued to be kind to us. There are still a few little tomatoes ripening in the garden, and green beans remain to be picked. For weeks there have been plenty of waving cosmos and bright zinnias, and the overgrown roses seem to like these cool October days, at least enough to surprise us with a sweet blossom here and there before winter comes. Best of all, the morning glories have bloomed at last. For months the vines have been sprawling over the garden fence and climbing the archway above the gate, and we have waited patiently for the cooler days of September to welcome their bloom. We have waited and waited. September came and went, and not one promising blue blossom.

Then, at last, October arrived. Helen Hunt Jackson's wonderful poem says that the suns and skies of June cannot compare to "October's bright blue weather." But for us, it was not the blue skies which we celebrated, but the glorious heavenly blue morning glories that decorated the edge of our garden. They are called "Heavenly Blue" for a reason. There is hardly another blue in nature to compare with these simple flowers, huge azure trumpets with a golden throat serenading the sunrise. For a week or two they have been gracing us. And the bees, too, have been thankful for them, making their last rounds before the flowers are gone at last. One afternoon a host of bumblebees flew in and out of heaven's blue, and in one great blossom I found a pair of them entwined—content, perhaps, to stay there forever.

That was not meant to be. Overnight a cold front swept through our valley, and when I stepped outside at dawn, the thermometer had just touched the freezing mark. The world seemed to shiver a bit with this brush of frost. It was not a hard frost. The marigolds and pineapple sage are still green and tall, and the tomatoes haven't given up, either. But, alas, the tender morning glories are drooping and shriveled. Now we will have to wait for next year to see such loveliness again. And the bees will have to look for heaven somewhere else.

Morning Glory

My love,
we cut across the grain of the year
in this season of angled light,
seeking one more moment of summer.
It is not ours to make, or will,
but sometimes it comes
as grace note
to the dwindling days.
One mellow day,
the sun smiles warm
upon this world of orange and gold,
and the soft air hums
with the gladness of bees who have found
a tapestry of morning glories
trimming our backyard fence with blue,
a color richer than sky and sea.
I will hold this vision,
keep coming to it,
that there is heaven in the world
to find,
some goodness lovely as a morning glory
whose center is a star,
a golden promise
I would share with you.

October

Ghoulie Girl

October is a delicious, joyous month, celebrated under a canopy of golds and maroons and the year's bluest sky. Sunday afternoon we picked apples at the local orchard. The wind was swirling and there was a nip in the air, but we came home with a bag full of Golden Delicious apples and the sweetness of autumn in our blood. We carved pumpkins into jack-o-lanterns, which will stand guard on our front steps this Friday night as a parade of children come to our door looking for "trick or treat" candy. And we have rigged up our Ghoulie Girl at the end of our kitchen sidewalk.

This has become an annual tradition. Usually sometime early in October our granddaughters start asking about "Ghoulie Girl," and so the supplies come down from the attic and the inflatable black cat and pumpkin emerge from the basement. An old nightgown and rubber gloves serve for the body and a broomstick for the arms. The face is an ugly mask attached to the post light, topped with an old wig and pointed hat. She looks enough like a witch to be scary, but we laugh merrily at her appearance.

Some communities are giving up the celebration of Halloween. Certain religious groups have an aversion to a holiday with roots in pagan worship and evil spirits. Others have a more pragmatic aversion to children running through the streets in the dark so that they can load up on candy. One area school system is encouraging a more generic "fall festival" instead. But the child in me remembers frosty nights and the shuffle of leaves, a bulging pillowcase and the smell of my breath behind a scary mask. And I still sometimes feel the shiver that comes from a moon peering through twisted branches, the wail of the wind, the possibility of something unknown lurking beyond the edges of my safe and familiar world. I want a candle inside a grinning pumpkin face to light up the night, at least for a moment. Though I am a child no more, I am glad for a Ghoulie Girl to remind me that joy can still turn away the darkness.

Ghoulie Girl

She stands guard,
a nightgowned sentinel
with crooked face and billowing dress,
watching the shadows for us.
We fashion this wild-haired spectre
out of cloth and sticks,
but also out of the old fears
that lurk in the helpless places
within us.
We know the night,
recognize the grim voices
that cry out from a cruel, embattled world,
hold our breath and cross our fingers
that the blind angel of fate
will fly on by.
And we are haunted by
our own shadow,
the one that rises in our sleepless nights,
the one we have not learned to love.
So in the season of failing light,
we set a little light to shine,

some twisted smile to grin a hope
into the night,
then call it joy that bends our fears away
when we are child again.

November

November

Bittersweet

The small creatures of the world know that a great change is happening as we swing into a New England November. There is less daylight to do the work of foraging and stockpiling for winter. The chipmunks scurry back and forth from the feeders, their cheeks swollen from the load of sunflower seeds they are carrying back to their underground caches. And the songbirds flit from bare branch to the residue of the summer garden in search of whatever may be left for them to eat. Around the edges of the yard, there is still plenty. The rose bushes are loaded with bright orange rosehips, and the winterberry bushes in front of the house are heavy with rows of red fruit. And everywhere, the woods are decorated with bittersweet vines.

    Most of the bittersweet in our region is an invasive plant which arrived in this country in the mid 1800s. It spirals around fence posts and climbs the highest trees in the forest to gather sunlight, and through the summer its green berries swell until they turn golden in autumn's cooler days. Then, one morning after a frost, those golden berries will explode and reveal, inside their yellow husks, deep crimson berries. This is nature's autumn décor, the color reserved for the gray days after the last leaves have fallen to the earth. We cut the vines and weave them into wreaths for the doors.

And in our dining room, they circle our ceiling chandelier and surround the table centerpiece, a colorful celebration of the dwindling year.

Those door wreaths are enjoyed by the birds, too, who eat the berries and scatter the seeds in places where we don't want the plants to grow. Underground their stringy orange roots begin to spread. Beware of digging them up or pulling them out, because even just a piece of root left in the ground can generate a new plant. And don't eat the berries by mistake. They are toxic to humans, even fatal. However, Native Americans used the plant for a variety of ailments, including reducing fever and pain in childbirth, causing vomiting, and as a skin ointment. They knew how to do it, and I don't. So this bitter-tasting plant I leave to the birds and chipmunks to eat, and for us to bring just a little color into these darkening days.

Bittersweet

Like golden pearls,
these little fruits bejewel
their woody vines
climbing, twisting upward,
along fence and forest trees,
growing strong in summer's light.
And now, in these sullen days,
through the fallowing of our land,
they claim an even brighter presence.
We admire their persistence,
curse it too,
for taking root where we would plant
some other thing more tame, less wild.
But it is noble for us all to persevere,
to stay the course in wintry days
that we may flower again another spring.
So we gather these branches, and remember
to find sweetness in the bitter times,
to be beautiful in our dying down,
to spread our roots in deeper soil.
We remember to be glad that
in the time of dark and cold,
the reddest berries show.

November

Wood, Split

The year is coming round full circle. These past days have been mild and soft, but the forecast promises that much colder air is on the way. I have been out by the woodpile, splitting some big logs into smaller pieces that will make our hearth fires on the coming cold nights. I do this with some care, as my wife discourages me from using any tools that have the potential of causing injury. This is because I have a reputation for being a somewhat clumsy handyman.

However, I actually have some experience with an axe. As a teenager, there was a huge elm tree in our back yard that fell victim to the plague of Dutch Elm Disease. My father thought it would be a good thing for a young man to get some exercise by chopping it up, providing us firewood at the same time. I learned then that elm is almost impossible to chop; its grain is twisted and stringy and when it grabs the blade of the ax, it won't let go. And it's not a great firewood anyway; it burns with a peculiar smell. But we had plenty of it, and it took me the better part of a summer before I gave up and let my father have it hauled away. Now I enjoy chopping wood, especially the satisfaction of feeling the axe head hit home so that the log falls cleanly apart. These are the pieces—oak and maple— that will burn red in our hearth in the winter days ahead.

We have a fire in us, too—the thing that burns in us with warmth and light in those cold, dark days. Hidden in us is a life that has grown through the green seasons—all those memories hidden inside, sometimes even unrecognized until something splits them open, reveals them to the light. They are both sweet and terrible, joys and sorrows, fueling in us some deep happiness or abiding anger. This week I unexpectedly remembered a football game in a neighbor's yard many, many years ago, where I, at the bottom of a pile, fell on a fumbled ball and felt my wrist crack under the weight of all those people on top of me. I rode home alone on a bicycle, tried to wish the pain away, was taken to the emergency room, fearing death. I remember little else, except waking up in my bed, arm bound in a cast, with my father sitting on a chair beside me, hand on my shoulder. It is in me, this wood for my fire.

Wood, Split

A flurry of leaves
and a west wind sings a winter song
as the ax is raised,
then arcs through the shining air
and thunks into the wood's heart.
The log cries out, falls apart,
split open, white, in the November sun.
Here is the secret center,
hidden for years while giving life
to a once-tall oak,
now revealed, seen, kept.
So we grow, too,
our memories stored
in the dark center of us,
every wound and wonder,
each sweet joy and buried sorrow,
the hallowed mornings and the night dreams,
the unspent wishes and the silent regrets,
the first kiss and the tendered hand,
the shared meal and the lonely walk in rain,
all there, all there,
deep at the wood's heart,
ready to be flame.

November

Birthday

It is a cold and quiet morning. In the southern sky a sliver of a moon hangs motionless as a line of geese make their hemline on the horizon. But this quiet morning belies the great speed of things. We are already in the fading days of November and the trees are mostly bare now. Wasn't it just summer? There is still an air conditioner in the window, needing to be stored in the attic. And yesterday my wife had to take a hair dryer to remove the hose frozen to the outdoor faucet on the north side of the house. Where has the time gone?

But the speed of our lives is nothing compared to the actual speed of our world. I've read that earth is rotating at about 1,000 miles per hour. For earth to circle the sun in a year, our planet must travel about 66,000 miles an hour. And the sun and our solar system itself is moving through our galaxy at a breakneck speed as well. One estimate is that the sun is dragging us all through the Milky Way galaxy at 483,000 miles per hour. And our galaxy itself is speeding outward from that initial bang at 1.3 million miles per hour, moving toward some mysterious concentration of matter in the faraway depths of the universe—something called "The Great Attractor."

At these enormous speeds, we should be flinging ourselves onto the earth and holding on for dear life. But gravity helps us out, and instead we walk peacefully through our quiet morning, forgetting altogether that we are infinitesimal specks in the vastness of a wildly expanding cosmos. But our specks, to us, our precious. This week my wife, Phyllis, has a major birthday, a celebration of her appearance on this planet. It feels like we have travelled too quickly to this milestone, but today I stop to marvel at a sliver of moon and a thread of singing geese and the wonder of this one, good life. What a ride!

Birthday

We ride through time and space
breathless from birth
at the speed of it all,
at the lives around us
which flicker for a moment
and fade away,
the echoes of billions of heartbeats
lost in the wake of our little years.
But we are here,
the glow of candles on a cake
reflecting in our eyes
to remind us that this one life
has been, for us, a shining light.
Though the world may sail into the darkness,
though stars may burn and die,
though this speck of cosmic dust may seem
as nothing in the great vastness,
She has lived with flowers in her heart,
rocked a baby in her arms
and nestled a squirrel in her hair,
flung herself into the sea
and dipped her fingers into earth
as if she could find there some timeless joy,

and laughed so wondrously
that for a moment the universe stood still
grateful that such a thing as Phyllis
could ever be.

November

A Song to Slip from the Heart

Tomorrow is Thanksgiving, and I am glad for it. We will gather family members—and maybe some others—around the table and reflect on this gift, which is life. Thanksgiving is a wonderful holiday—perhaps more than any other—because it is just about being together. It is also a time to feel the tender spirits around us of those who have shared their lives with us. As we pause to say grace, they linger at the edges of the room, their voices whispering through our silence, saying things like "Did you put sausage in the stuffing?" and "Look how big your granddaughter is already!" and "I love you."

    When I was a little boy I would awaken on Thanksgiving morning to the aroma of roasting turkey wafting through the house, because my mother and father had risen before dawn to stuff the bird and lace it up for the oven. This was a ritual of love. So we will rise on Thursday—though not quite so early—and repeat that ritual for another year, and my mother and father will be there, and not. Yesterday we planted daffodil and tulip bulbs in the cold earth, perhaps the last mild day before a winter storm arrives today. This, too, is a ritual bound to our Thanksgiving feast—of planting and harvest, of making a pact with those who have been and those who are yet to come. We live in memory and hope. For that, we are grateful.

A Song to Slip from the Heart

Go there
in the sullen days,
when the heart is dark as November
and there is no respite from the cold.
Go there,
and find some little thing
to hold in your shaking hand,
one last red leaf,
or a blue feather from a morning bird,
or an acorn with some life in it.
Lift it up to the sky,
which may be silent and heavy with clouds,
but it is high, and worth seeing,
for you must look up if you would be a priest
who bears this offering.
And then you will wait for the song
to slip from your heart,
where you have locked it up,
a song that remembers
what it is to be a child running in grass,
a song of seasons and snow and rain,
a song of laughter and tender voices.
Suddenly it will be there,

and if you have ever known love,
known some sweet kiss or felt arms around,
or felt the stronger, stranger love
like a flame tearing at the darkness,
or a wounded forgiveness,
then this song will be a worthy anthem,
and true as leaf or feather or seed.
And then light will settle around you,
and in you a joy will take its root,
and you will be saved by this one,
truest, deepest prayer,
lifted up, like a wild and holy incantation:
Thank you. Thank you.

December

December

Red

Last week the town crew was out all day, attaching evergreens and great red bows to the hundreds of lampposts lining Main Street. It was an expensive project, to be sure, considering the cost of all the materials as well as the paid hours necessary to do the job. But it looks beautiful to have the town decked out for the season, and most of us deem it worth the cost. This Saturday night is the annual holiday stroll, with all the shops open, a horse drawn wagon for the kids, a tree-lighting ceremony and a gingerbread house contest.

But I am struck by all those red bows fluttering in the December breeze. In these dim, gray days, they proclaim a joy that captures us, lifts us out of the year's doldrums. December, this colorless month, is edged with red as a gift, calling us to celebrate even in the dark times. We see it out the kitchen window as a pair of cardinals wing their way to our bird feeder, a glory in feathers. By the front door, the winterberry bushes are covered with red berries the size of marbles, and over across the yard the holly seems to be singing the old medieval carol: "The holly bears a berry as red as any blood!"

Maybe that is why red makes the heart leap. It is the color of our blood, the essential substance that pulses in and out of our hearts, giving us life.

Often when we see blood's red it is a sign of danger. There has been an accident, an injury, a wound that must be tended. Our blood best does its work unseen. But the red around us in the world reminds us of that hidden source of life, the primal red that is within all human beings. It is a call to embrace life, to wonder at this secret that hides within us. It is the force that turns winter away, that reminds us that we are all family. It makes us want to sing.

Red

In the wakening light
of earliest morning
a flash of red outside the window
promises something beautiful
in these grim days.
It is just a bird seeking food,
but also something to stir the heart.
It is rose and berry and blood,
a wild and feathered miracle
that flies like joy.
We shall hang scarlet bows
on wreath and mantel,
deck our tables with holly,
its red berries winking a secret
to us in our passing.
This red is in us,
the life of life,
the thing that will help us to endure
the darkest winters,
the brightness that binds us
to friend and stranger,
the color of miracles in a gray time
that make us fly like joy.

December

Christmas Tree

December for us is a season of rituals involving food, decorations, and the keeping of time. In this dark season around the winter Solstice, these rituals serve as a reminder that life not only endures the dark and cold seasons, but gives us joy. This weekend we headed out to get our Christmas tree, something we have come to do on the first weekend in December since our children were young. As a child, my family acquired a Christmas tree from a lot in the city, chosen from an assortment of trees that were probably cut down in September. And we always put our tree up on my sister's birthday, Dec. 18. My wife's family religiously did their tree on Christmas Eve, to the accompaniment of a turkey dinner and Christmas carols on the stereo.

But we have come to like having the tree up a little longer, enjoying its magic even as the needles begin to grow brittle and fall to the floor. We have not yet succumbed to the temptation of purchasing an artificial tree, whose needles will never fall. I cherish the fresh, pungent scent of a balsam, even when tromping through the meadow in search of the perfectly-shaped tree takes place in the middle of a monsoon. Such was the case on Saturday. But we had already planned the outing, and the grandchildren were eager to get their tree. This annual attraction is sweeter because at Joe's Christmas Tree Farm, they always have a bonfire going so that kids can cook a hot dog or roast a marshmallow before tying the tree to the top of the car and heading home. Saturday the hot dog buns were soggy, and the marshmallows were covered with ashes because in the rain, there wasn't much of a blaze for cooking. But a good time was had by all, and finally we located just the prettiest tree we've ever had. And I, with my saw, knelt on the saturated earth and cut it down. Shortly afterward, my wife spotted an even prettier tree, but that one will have to wait until next year.

Our Puritan ancestors had no use for Christmas trees. They denounced them as pagan, a stain on the holiness of their religious holiday. They banned them in New England for a while. I prefer Martin Luther's take on things. It is said that he was walking in the woods at night and saw stars shining through the branches of a fir. Such beauty, he thought, should be in every home. And it still is, in ours.

Christmas Tree

Hands sticky with sap,
fresh from the cutting wound,
I set the tall fir inside the window,
where its lights will be seen
by those standing outside in the cold.
And here, inside, near a glowing hearth,
where we sit in the darkness
of a December night,
some magic will shine on us, too.
We hang the ornaments of our history
on these fragrant branches,
the glow of memory reflected
in glitter and glass.
But perhaps it would be enough
to do as my father did,
in the last of his Christmases,
forgoing the balls and garlands,
and hanging just a few lights
to illuminate his quiet celebration.
There in the darkness of that year
he fell asleep to something like stars
shining in these tender boughs,
a promise in winter
of something evergreen.

December

Hearth Fire

The Christmas season is full of old traditions and folklore. Their origins may be lost or forgotten, but we continue to savor them as a rich connection with those who once shared their Christmases with us. My family would go to the home of my Aunt Anna and Uncle Daniel, who was Swedish by background. Aunt Anna would always make rice pudding, a Swedish tradition, and she would stir an almond in it. She assured us that the person fortunate enough to get the almond in their bowl of pudding would be the next one in the family to get married. This was not necessarily a pleasing prospect for a young boy, and fortunately, I never got the almond. My wonderful Aunt Anna may have also been the one to tell us how the animals in the forest would kneel down at midnight on Christmas Eve, and assure us that the bees who had gone into hibernation would awaken, no matter the weather, and hum the 100th Psalm. It seemed far-fetched even then, but I dreamed of sneaking out into the woods to see if any part of this tale could be true. Our world should be filled with such dreams.

And where I love to dream best is by the fire. We have a fireplace in our living room. The house was built in 1834, and at that time the living room was the kitchen, and the hearth was the place where meals were prepared. The chimney crane bearing an iron pot still extends over the fire, unused for many years, and a beehive oven next to the hearth could be filled with hot coals to heat up the bricks inside for baking. Over the years, my three little boys all hid in there, and I smile still when I walk past. But although there is no more cooking in the fireplace, I still light fires on autumn and winter nights and feel comforted by its warmth and hypnotized by its firelight. Perhaps it is a primal thing that has united human beings from the dawn of time—the attraction of a fire. It is the place of human gatherings, of feasts and family, the place we go to find respite from the terrors of the night. It is the thing, strangely, that both symbolizes our passions and brings us peace.

For years it has been my tradition to start each year's Christmas fire with the cut up trunk of last year's Christmas tree. By the hearth on Christmas morning, I feel connected to all that has gone before in my life—the rice pudding and the almond, the hands held around the table, the carols sung in the snow by the front door, the stockings hung from the mantel. I see faces smiling at me from the flickering flames, would rather not move from the place where I may read and dream and fall asleep.

Hearth Fire

Old Hestia, the ancient god of hearth,
missed all the festal gatherings
of the great divinities,
shunned lofty Olympus
just to stay at home
for duty's sake, tending to the fire.
She was perhaps the wisest,
humblest of the gods,
this keeper of the hearth
where weary sojourners could come
to warm themselves with food and flame.
And still to fire and hearth we come
to be where we may see
some spirit dancing in the flames
calling us from fear to faith,
or yet more simply,
to teach us constancy,
to give us some small peace
where we may join the cat curled up,
the dog stretched out,
here where love's best gift
is just to stir the embers.

December

Somewhere a Star

Today is Christmas Eve. In anticipation of the family being together to celebrate this wonderful holiday, I was in the kitchen last night amid a flurry of flour and sugar and lots and lots of butter. The cookies are done, and the next round of baking will be in the wee hours tomorrow morning when I make the Swedish tea ring in honor of my grandfather and fry up the Ferden (sugared German doughnuts) in memory of my father, whose cast iron aebleskiver pan is hauled out once a year for this purpose.

But tonight we will go to the old white church where a host of costumed children will put on the annual Christmas Pageant. One of the tinsel-haloed cherubs sitting by the manger will fall asleep, and another will make faces in the spotlight. One of the Wise Men will forget the words to his verse of "We Three Kings," and a shepherd will be caught with his finger up his nose. The Baby Jesus will cry his lungs out in spite of his parents' efforts to render him groggy with milk an hour before the play. All of this is as it should be. Around midnight we will gather in the church again to light candles and sing "Silent Night." As we sing I will be thinking of the father whom I held in my arms a few days ago. He had just lost his son in a terrible car accident and was inconsolable. There will be no silent night for him, no "calm and bright," no heavenly peace.

The mystery of Christmas, though, is that we perform these ancient rites in spite of heartbreak and loss, in the midst of a world that is fractured by violence and hatred, because we need to believe that something bigger—perhaps Love itself—holds us. Sometimes it feels like a dream. Last Sunday during the carol sing in our church we all joined in a chorus of "White Christmas." The snow was falling gently outside the tall, clear glass windows in the old building, and it just seemed right, even though it is certainly not a religious song. But it stirs something deep in us—this dream of a world bright and shining and full of love. It is one of the most spiritual yearnings of all, the thing that can make us good. In the end, it is really not something bigger that holds us, but something very small. It is the crying baby in the straw, the sleeping angel, the dream I wish for every weeping father—that even the smallest love is stronger than all the darkness, all the hurt.

Somewhere a Star

Somewhere a star
gleams in the darkest night,
pure as the promise
that once glittered
in a Bethlehem sky.
It is for us who journey
on a lonely road,
or who have forgotten
where we are going.
It shines where no other beauty
can be seen,
a mystery and a wonder,
a cosmic explosion that to us
is just a point of light
in our tiny, shadowed world,
a little thing to follow
when our sun has set.
Sometimes that star
is all we have,
the thing on a dark and holy night
that kindles a spark of hope in us—
unlikely as it may seem—
reminds us that love invades the world,
shines a light that leads us home.

December

The Last Day

There is nothing special about this day, really. In the life of the planet, it is just another turn, one which completes a single orbit around our small star. The life here goes on as it did yesterday. The sparrows chattering in the forsythia bush along the edge of the yard know nothing about a new year. They will not be making resolutions or wondering what news will shatter their peace. They will scuttle around under the feeders for stray seed and huddle together in the cold night and wait for dawn, as they did yesterday.

But we are different. We mark time on calendars, remember the numbered years of our lives. We come to this night hoping to a find a doorway to something new, different. No matter that the earth is getting warmer, or that human creatures still seem to try to solve their problems with violence, or that the shadows of death hang over everything we love. We hold our breath, and in the pause, believe in goodness.

Today I arise before dawn and take two dogs out for their morning walk. Our feet crunch through the fallen leaves as we climb a hill behind the cemetery; and then in a grassy meadow I stop while the dogs go sniffing in the bushes. I am suddenly aware of the silence all around me. There is not the breath of a wind, and the world seems to stand stock-still. But I listen closely and hear a barely discernible distant sound. It is a hum—perhaps the drone of cars speeding past on a highway, I think. Or is it inside me, the throb and pulse of blood pushing through my arteries, the thing giving me life? Or the primal thrum of the universe, the music of the spheres? A dog barks down the street, and overhead somewhere a hawk cries, hungry for morning, and the quiet returns. It is a sweet silence, this. The world, my world, holding its breath, as something new waits just over the hill.

The End of a Year

Sparrows chatter
to greet this cold morning,
and I fling a handful of seed
across the barren ground.
Months from now
I will kneel here,
lay seeds in fallow earth
so that something green might grow.
But now the seed is gift,
a tender offering to the feathered ones,
tossed into the doorway of the year
as hope and promise
that we will make it through
this looming winter together.
Somewhere fireworks splash across the sky,
and lovers kiss away their fears,
a road curves off into a new year
as infants sleep beneath wishful stars.
But I will walk on frozen earth
and pause to listen to my heartbeat,
which is today a song of gratitude
that I am here

in this wonder of a life
where birds still sing,
where sunrise makes the sky
into a rose.

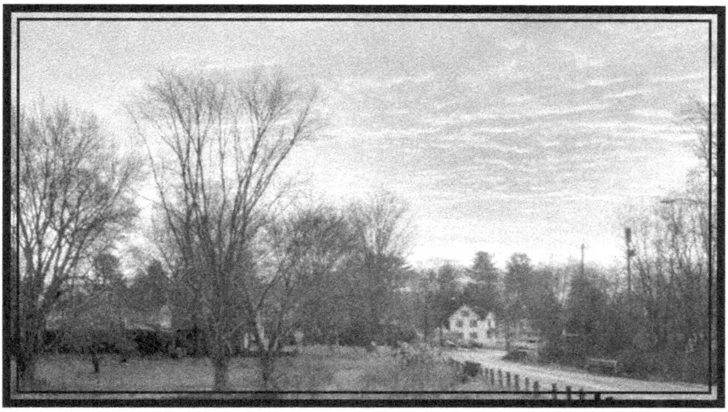

CPSIA information can be obtained
at www.ICGtesting.com
Printed in the USA
BVHW030333271219
567938BV00019B/48/P